MAGIC . . .
THE SIMPLE TRUTH

Magic . . .
The Simple Truth

Alchemy for Today's World—
The Real Magic Course

Sylvia Bennett

Library of Congress Number:		2004097910
ISBN :	Hardcover	1-4134-6980-9
	Softcover	1-4134-6979-5

This book was printed in the United States of America.

To order additional copies of this book, contact:
Xlibris Corporation
1-888-795-4274
www.Xlibris.com
Orders@Xlibris.com
24035

CONTENTS

INTRODUCTION

THE REAL MAGIC Course is a course in spiritual alchemy that I created in the early 1980s and taught for many years. This Course evolved from my own spiritual search and from my inability to find a spiritual path that resonated with my spiritual longing. In the early 1970s I was a disillusioned 1960s political radical looking for spiritual revolution. I longed for authentic change, deep and elemental. I longed for a teacher who could help me. Other women fantasized about men; I fantasized about mystery schools. I studied metaphysics and ancient religions, and everywhere I looked, from Don Juan to Yogananda, I found intimations of the teacher and school I longed for but no coherent path I could follow. I wanted to learn to transmute energy, and I wanted to access the essential universal principles that exist in the ancient mystery religions. I set out to create the teacher and the school that I wanted and was unable to find.

My interest in spirituality, in alchemy, and in metaphysics is a part of me that has always existed. It is on a par with my childhood devotion to Jesus—a part of my nature and intrinsic to my earliest childhood memories. I was a very religious little girl, a child mystic. I spent my early life pursuing art, poetry, metaphysics, and music. I am the mother of two grown children. At diverse times in my life I've been a beatnik, a painter, sculptor, poet, jazz singer, songwriter, mother, and radical feminist. My creation of the Real Magic Course is a natural extension of who and what I am. I couldn't *not* create it.

I am clairsentient, which means I have a gift or talent for receiving and comprehending data that is seen and heard beyond the ordinary range of senses and is often referred to as the sixth sense, the Sight, or extrasensory perception. I am a spiritual channel. I channeled teachings from the Christ Consciousness, incorporated them into my life as true and created classes from those teachings.

Channeling is hypercognition—an accelerated frequency of cognition that allows data to be received and processed in extra-sensory ways. Information is received and processed faster than the speed of sound—faster even than thought—for a flow of high-frequency spiritual vibration stops the energy of the *interpretive* mind. It does not stop the energy of the inquiring mind. There is always a dialogue. Channeling is God's Word appearing as spiritual inspiration, song, poetry, images, ideas, and words of wisdom from the God-mind to the human mind. There are no words to describe the sense of vast, sentient space and light, the awesome intelligence and love that accompany such communion. Also, there are no words to describe the self-doubt that often arises. There is no place to hide from such sentient truth and when it lifts away, you can feel utterly alone. It challenges you to become so true that you are never alone, and contradictions like alone-not alone no longer exist for you.

As an artist and creative jazz improviser I was familiar with the experience of being overtaken by a force greater, more intelligent, and truer than my everyday self, so I did not experience channeling as strange, awesome, or extra-ordinary. But it felt very private, and I am a very private person. For that reason, I had trouble accepting the spiritual phenomenon of channeling when it first appeared in my life in the late 1960's. Channeling was very popular and I was very judgmental about what I perceived as a lack of discernment in the New Age pop culture—it seemed as if anything "channeled" was proclaimed as true simply because it had been channeled. At the same time I was receiving, through channeling, specific information from teachers of vast and awesome intelligence. I felt really frightened by this contradiction. I was fastidious. I did not want to reveal myself to a world that I feared would treat me as the latest New Age commodity. A friend who was following my process during this, my dark night of the soul, once told me I was still a beatnik artist at heart and that I was experiencing the age-old struggle of the artist versus the supermarket. At the same time that I feared the spiritual market place, I also felt compelled to teach and compelled to be true to my essential nature.

In order to come to terms with this paradox and balance my increasingly schizophrenic existence, I had to accept that channeling is a natural process and something all human beings do. Communion with God is part of the human structure of being and just as all people can learn to play the piano but not all people can play the piano with artistry, so not all people are gifted *wave transmitters*. Channeling is the reason why ancient shamans were referred to as "two-headed". To exist as a two-headed woman, I had to get tough and grounded. I did. I got tough and I got strong, and as I became an experienced teacher, I began to experience a state that was both passionate conviction and nonchalance—nonattachment. I learned to impart the Teachings without being attached to what people did with them.

I had to teach. My own visionary nature and the quality of channeled information I was receiving were compelling me to teach people that human beings have the ability to transmute energy. "Transmute" means structural and molecular change. Primal change—something even beyond transformation—or beyond the present use of that word. Being a visionary, I believe it is possible to change human nature and the human condition, and I believe the planet is calling out for us to create these changes. And the most vital, the most radical change we are now being called to create is the change from an anthropomorphic, patriarchal way of *believing* to a more feminine, multidimensional, holistic, non-dual way of *being*.

The Hermetic teachings are the source of alchemy. These teachings came to me through my relationship with the Divine Sophia. She was my awakening. She came to me and opened my heart to my truest Self. She taught me to think in a Hermetic Way or to think *multidimensionally* in a way I would describe as esoteric and creative rather than psycho-mental/linear. She is the Mother of Alchemy, the Logos, the Feminine Christ Consciousness. And Sophia is *Presence*. She is a living Being and as She approached me

I felt for the first time in my life, *loved*. She taught me Love and I gave her all the devotion my hungry little heart had been longing to give. I love Her. I asked Her what She wanted of me and She told me to *be* the "Book of Sophia" and this, I believe is what she is asking of all of us today—that we become Her Book . . . Her hands, Her voice, Her Heart embodied on earth as a single point of focus . . . Love. She introduced me to Mary, Mother of Jesus, and Mary Magdalene, both of them expressions of the Incarnate Sophia. My Sisters. But since I am not here to focus on and teach a new system of belief, I have never taught Sophiology, and rather than teach about Her I have searched for ways to teach people that rather than be true to any form of belief, be true, instead, to their own highest aspirations, their own truest Self. And in doing this I believe I am honoring everything She is, for She *is* direct experience, radical experience, and She needs no go-betweens. She is Present in everything I teach but I had to find my own Tao, my own Way to teach what I was learning.

In searching for the Tao of teaching, I conceived the idea of a Mystery School—not so much a physical place as a state of being—an eclectic and evolving way to bring vision into alignment with technology and create a comprehensive spiritual path. My vision of a Mystery School was strong, but I chose not to promote the idea or advertise myself in any way. I didn't want to make my spirituality a business venture. I approached the Course as a work of art. I let it evolve and create its own forms. I hoped by not advertising to attract a few political or social rebels, skeptics, creative artists, and like-minded friends. I could not identify with mainstream spirituality. I was disturbed by the overuse of words like "abundance" and "choice" in the emerging New Age culture. I worked in a New Age bookstore/cultural center and was appalled by what I perceived as avarice, as greed in the name of God. Yet I was an advocate for freedom. All the same, more does not mean better, and abundance does not mean excess. I was an advocate for *Small is Beautiful* and I believed that teaching my own spiritual philosophy would be a small, radical, intelligent, and creatively satisfying aspect of my life.

It didn't work that way. I became the spiritual teacher I had once longed for. My approach to esoteric teaching appealed to people. I had underestimated people's desire for Reality. I have never advertised but people came and keep coming, and I continue to learn from them. I attracted wonderful people who demanded that I give them my best and catalyzed me into real and ongoing growth. They taught me how to teach.

I called the Course *Real Magic* because I wanted to convey a sense of authenticity and immediacy. The word "real" does not mean "only". Real Magic is not the only Way of transformation. It is *a* way, not *the* way. I have been teaching for over twenty years. Just as I once felt compelled to create classes, I now feel compelled to write. I've come to feel in dismantling the Course to create a book, that nothing can be taught except through direct experience and that a book is just a book and a book is, in the end, only literature. So I don't know if I've written a book that will teach, but I hope I've written a praise poem, a book that will inspire and help others to find their own Path of Light.

I wish to acknowledge the inexpressible gratitude I feel toward my beloved teachers: Sophia, the Feminine Christ Consciousness who embodies the Beauty and Intelligence of God; St. Germain—master alchemist and gentleman *extraordinaire;* and Jesus, master physicist and the best big brother any frightened child ever had.

Gratitude to Krishnamurti for the beauty of his intelligence. He wasn't so much teacher as he was pure *Being.* He was unable to depart from pure truth so he left the translating of that truth to spiritual worker-bees like me—he just told it like it is.

Gratitude to the Sufis for the absolute Beauty of God to be found in the Sufi tradition of poet as spiritual teacher.

I dedicate this book to the three anonymous adepts who wrote *The Kybalion.* Their attempt to preserve and transmit ancient Hermetic Principles into a universal language has inspired many seekers, like me, who weren't sure what they were looking for until they discovered this gem of a book. *The Kybalion* cannot be credited to any one author and I don't want to speculate about who might have written it. It was a labor of love. And it inspired me to dedicate this book to the "ministers of Love" who have kept the Hermetic Flame alive through countless centuries.

O, let not the Flame die out! Cherished age after age—fed by pure ministers of Love—let not the Flame die out! (The Kybalion)

Dedicated with infinite gratitude to all Keepers of the Flame.

I dedicate this book to my children and to all the very fine teachers who have come into my life in the form of students. Thank you for blessing my existence, for blessing the earth, and for blessing each other. God bless you. Walk in Peace and Beauty in a World restored to Harmony.

Sylvia Bennett
Bellingham, WA. 2003

PART ONE

ALCHEMY AND
THE WESTERN ESOTERIC TRADITION

Behold! Thy Soul is a Living Star.

Egyptian masters say the Soul is a Living Star. Bring the Living Star into the dark and

Illumination will transmute the dark. This is the simple truth. This is Real Magic.

A WESTERN HEART

AN INTELLECTUAL FRIEND of mine, an anthropologist, once said to me, "Your version of magic is too simple to be believed." And I said, "Yes, it is, isn't it . . . it's the simple truth." The complete art and technology of magic could be stated in a few simple sentences but no one would believe it or be able to utilize it. The simple thesis of magic is that if you take the most powerful thing you have (attention) and focus it through the most powerful force in the universe (intention) you can create energies that will restructure your subtle and physical world. Now, that is simply and literally true.

Notice I said *your* world, not *the* world. You can influence and change the structure of your world by changing the structure of your self. But you cannot change another person and you cannot change God. If you consider that God is molecular integrity and God is a vast mystery, the eternal and infinite energy from which all form is created, a supremely intelligent and conscious *Intention*, then only God can change God and all you can truly know is your own piece of that. My piece of that is a combination of philosophy and technology that I call alchemy, the simple practice of which is called magic.

What is alchemy? The thesis of alchemy is, "As above, so below". Alchemy evolved from the Hermetic belief that there is a divine intention *(as above)* at the root of all created form, and human beings *(so below)* carry a spark of this divine intention. This spark gives human beings a capacity to reach superconsciousness—the Christ Consciousness. If God is a vast living consciousness and humanity a living star, a spark from the living Fire of God, then human beings have within them, in that spark, the Secret of Fire—the ability to transmute energy.

God and humanity have an agreement: humanity will learn wisdom. Humanity might stumble and fall time after time, but humanity is hard-wired to seek out God and find wisdom. And in the end, God and humanity merge in essence as One wisdom consciousness—Sophia. Inherent in this philosophy is the belief that this transformation is the ultimate desire or dream of God.

The Real Magic Course is founded on this thesis and on the knowledge that human beings have within themselves the ability to transmute energy. This course in applied alchemy teaches you to transmute energy and restructure your world. The Course is a path of learning to understand and utilize a technology that in common language is referred to as "magic". This is essentially simple. But your past, your beliefs and your questions make it complex. To go from complexity to simplicity requires some understanding of the structure of a thing. The fundamental structure of The Real Magic Course lies in my relationship with alchemy. If I had not been thoroughly grounded in an understanding of alchemy, I couldn't have created the Course.

This first section of the book is not about theories and it is not a psychological attempt to explain magic. It is about how to understand the origins of The Real Magic Course by understanding alchemy within my lineage, the Western Esoteric Tradition. I spent years on a mission—as if I had a magnet at the top of my head and it was pointed unerringly toward *something* and I was compelled to follow. I had a compelling desire to learn *how* to transmute energy so that I could teach people. Magic is Divine Intelligence in Action. Magic is a word that describes both the action of Creation and what that action produces. It is a sacred technology. I knew that since magic is a technology, it could be learned and taught. In order to approach it as technology, I turned to the study of alchemy.

I didn't study or practice alchemy in a traditional or occult sense of the word. The *Kybalion*, an anonymous and lovely little book on the Hermetic Teachings, declares that alchemy is a *mental art,* an art created for the purpose of changing *consciousness,* and that is the spirit in which I have pursued the study of alchemy. I don't use any rituals in the Course, and I don't use the language and symbols usually associated with alchemy. Alchemy is the art of using energy to change energy, of using consciousness to change consciousness. A mental art. Alchemy is often a solitary path, and I was very much a loner, looking for the deep spiritual essence of something I called Reality. Capital *R*. Also, I am not an apologist for occultism because that is not the kind of knowledge I have pursued.

My spiritual insights began with my search for a spiritual alternative to orthodox, *exoteric* Christianity. I was not attracted to the Eastern religions. I am Western. In my search I found many mystics, psychologists, teachers, and writers, and many of my peers, focused on Eastern religions as if the West had no great wisdom tradition. I resented that for I felt passionately Western in my spiritual sensitivity—as if my bones, blood, and sinew had been forged in the beauty, passion, and poetry of Wales, Ireland, Africa, Egypt and the Mediterranean. I studied the Bible and Hebrew teachings. I read the Koran and the Sufis, and I studied ancient history, Renaissance Europe, Celtic Mysteries, St. Germain, Shakespeare, Jesus and Sophia.

I was running into a kind of spiritual class snobbery in some of the spiritual people I was meeting. In their recognition of me as a spiritual seeker, they invariably referred me to the writings of Eastern gurus and to Western psychologists. They questioned the spiritual validity of Alchemy, Kabbalah, and other Western metaphysical and esoteric concepts. This kind of snobbery among people who had been referred to me as spiritually authentic was very disappointing and made me determined to find intelligence and authenticity in the Western traditions. Actually it made me determined to *find* the Western Tradition.

I was discovering that pre-Christian spirituality was generally defined within pop psychology, shamanism, and witchcraft. Shamanism had a fairly prestigious audience because it was mysterious and male and had been written up by some renowned anthropologists. Witchcraft and shamanism had the same roots, and I was drawn to study witchcraft because I was a feminist. Being primarily female, witchcraft had a very bad press but I researched it simply because it was oriented toward a female deity, and as a religion, was earth-centered and focused on holistic healing. I explored the emerging goddess studies but found that the emphasis on separation in the emerging feminist goddess consciousness was not resonant with my vision. I was unable to conceive of a Divine Mother as separate from a Divine Father. And even twin deities, a Mother/Father concept, was too religious, too anthropomorphic for my taste. I believed that a focus on integration and not separation was crucial for the health of the world. You must remember that this was in the 1960s and early 1970s. The world has changed so much since then that integration is now the focus of a new creation-centered spirituality that did not exist at that time.

I had no sure definition of my vision but I had a compelling sense of purpose. That sense of purpose was focused fully in the Western Spirit even though I had bitterly rejected the Christianity of my youth, and also rejected shamanism and psychology. I couldn't connect with any orthodox Eastern religion as a spiritual life path. I was feeling torn apart by all the contradictions between my insights and what I was being told I should be pursuing. In rejecting the East and rejecting psychology it would seem that I might have been truly lost and rudderless. I was not. I often felt desperate and frightened and very inadequate but I never felt any lack of purpose. I was frustrated. I was obsessed with Freedom and I wanted direct experience. I wanted to experience what the face of God felt like, smelled and tasted like. Like Einstein, I wanted to know God's thoughts.

I explored the esoteric West as a realm of mystery and beauty, of higher physics, real magic, real wisdom, and God. In turning to the esoteric traditions, I was responding to an overwhelming divine inspiration. I was looking for the universality in the teachings, a truth beyond belief, beyond ideology, and, although I did not realize it at the time, even beyond concepts. As I studied esoteric systems, I was looking behind the dense and sometimes disturbing ideologies and the often deliberate obscurity of the symbolism and writing styles and into the universal principles that gave rise to the ideologies. I wasn't looking for a religion or a belief system. The Real Magic Course is not about any particular spiritual belief or system. I created my own system and the Course is designed to help you create your own system. All the same, the Western Esoteric Tradition is the place of my most cherished influences. Studying traditions such as Alchemy; Mystery Schools like the Greek and the Hermetic Egyptian; Islamic Sufis; Welsh and Irish Mysteries; the Hebrew Kabbalah; the Theosophists and Krishnamurti, satisfied the place of yearning in my mind and heart. My teachers Sophia, Jesus, and St. Germain are very much associated with the Western Mystery Tradition.

Just as there are many guru's, prophets, teachers, and systems within systems in the Eastern traditions, so the Western Esoteric Tradition is a fascinating collection of knowledge and wisdom from many diverse, interesting, sometimes wild and wonderful, sometimes fantastic, but very creative, prophets and teachers. I cannot attempt in this book to explore in-depth any one particular tradition or describe any of these amazing teachers. There are many books in existence about these traditions and teachers, and I have included a bibliography for anyone interested in further studies.

THE WESTERN ESOTERIC TRADITION AND PATHWORKING

It is unfortunate that the words alchemy and magic have become synonymous with the word "occult" because this word has become synonymous with dark supernatural forces. *Occult* is from a Greek word meaning hidden, and refers to knowledge that is subtle, nonverbal, and not easy to come by. It refers to subtle truths about God and human life, especially in regard to the power of human consciousness and the human psyche. In the esoteric traditions, occult refers to silent or *veiled* knowledge. This does not mean that the knowledge is secret; it means *silent.* Such knowledge cannot be theorized about or intellectualized; it must be experienced intuitively and as direct revelation.

Esoteric is another word that has come to be associated with the darker connotations of the word "occult". Esoteric refers specifically to the world of abstract ideas—art, literature, philosophy, music, higher mathematics, physics, spiritual doctrines—and I would include computer science as an esoteric study. The word "esoteric" indicates any system of knowledge that is understood by a group of initiates who are drawn to that system by their own nature. An esoteric system creates its own language and its own means of subtle communication; it creates its own *thought process.*

The Real Magic Course is an esoteric system. My idea for the teaching format evolved from the esoteric Mystery School tradition. The Mystery School was a place where spiritually gifted students could study the teachings of the spiritual masters. It was a place where teachers were trained and mastery was sought. This Mystery Tradition gave rise to the Western Esoteric Tradition—a tradition of universal spiritual studies and practices that are hard-wired to the Western mind and which evolved from esoteric Christianity, Greek and Egyptian Mysteries, the Hermetic teachings, and the Hebrew Kabbalah.

The Hebrew Tree of Life has become the classic example of the Western esoteric path. The word "kabbalah", in Hebrew, means collection. It also has a more subtle or *esoteric* translation meaning, "received, or having been received" and of course this implies received from God. The Kabbalah is made up of many books of Hebrew metaphysics and mysticism. During the Middle Ages, the Tree of Life, as it was translated in Europe from the collected mystery teachings of the Hebrew masters, became a major source of esoteric studies. In the nineteenth century esoteric groups such as the Golden Dawn, the Rosicrucians, the Inner Light Society, and the Theosophists, the word Kabbalah came to be associated with the Tree of Life and the Tarot.

The Tree of Life is a clear example of what, in the Western Tradition is referred to as *pathworking.* Pathworking is an esoteric teaching concept. It consists of consciously following a systematic series of spiritual practices, rather than learning a system of religious *beliefs*. The practices, used in combination with certain spiritual principles—not beliefs; *principles*—set in motion the energies of change.

Because the Western esoteric systems are not focused on following a particular belief or lineage, they are eclectic and emphasize autonomy and self-accountability. This does not mean the traditions don't require and respect teachers. The practices, like all spiritual practices are focused on shattering the ego and require an experienced teacher or guide. If you are a loner like me, you need a very powerful spiritual intention or calling and a powerful love for the Mystery of God. I was in a sense protected by my devotion to Sophia. The esoteric path creates itself from following one's *conscious* choices, paying *conscious* attention to the practices and to what manifests in the student's life from doing those practices. It is a path of *deliberation,* of deliberate choice and direct experience, of awareness and of *revelation.* By committing to the practices, the student comes to an awareness and understanding of the universal Truth that created those practices. This kind of path, a path of autonomy, is rooted in a desire to be true to one's self. I have heard so many of my students say they were longing to give themselves to something elemental and true. The rigorous discipline of autonomy requires a deep longing for freedom, for connection with the Self, and a desire for commitment and radical change. Real Magic is radical. It requires radical trust and determined effort—and courage. It is a path that leads to faith in a divine universe because it allows you to experience the workings of that divine universe in your own life experience until you know that there is nothing else.

An esoteric path, whether East or West, is different from an exoteric religious path. The path of any exoteric religion is based on orthodoxy, a practice of clear-cut beliefs, moral rules and judgments, of self-restraint rather than self-knowledge. The exoteric way of life is often easier in practice than an esoteric path because the rules and road maps are clear-cut and based on lineage and hierarchy, on accepted religious beliefs and on accepted social and moral values. An orthodox path tells you what to believe and promises you safety if you follow those beliefs. A path of orthodox belief can soothe, heal, and comfort the fearful, but belief can fixate fear, hold it in place, and hold one in the belief that fear is real. The path of orthodox belief is a fixed path and transformation is not part of orthodox religious experience except as defined within those beliefs.

Transformation often requires letting go of beliefs. It is focused on the transmutation of fear and the creation of that which is fearless. Transformation requires a path. It is not possible to take one class or workshop then walk away and incorporate into your life all of your potential wisdom or truth. Conscious pathwork is a labyrinth, a spiral, a circle that allows you come face-to-face with your potential for grace and miracle—and also to come face-to-face with your deepest fears and transform them. Students who have journeyed through the Real Magic Course more than once say that each journey is a new experience that reveals more truth. Students have said that walking through the Course the first time gets you ready to take the Course. This is true of any system of conscious pathwork. Conscious living is a continually unfolding path. Enhanced self-awareness, a sense of deep creative responsibility and a sense of being truly alive on a beautiful planet within a miraculous and divine universe becomes personal, an authentic, deeply spiritual, constant and *simple* way of life.

PATHS OF TRANSFORMATION

Esoteric systems that utilize the concept of conscious pathwork believe that there are several—usually *nine*—levels of consciousness through which a student must journey on the path to freedom. Transformation happens as the *polarities*, the contradictions between fear and faith—or you could say the disparity between ego (matter) and spirit—are transformed in each level or sphere of consciousness. Transformation occurs gradually as the student moves through the levels. There is a belief in each tradition that transformation is accomplished through the activity and guidance of a *tenth* aspect of consciousness, the Superconscious or high self, the Christ

Consciousness, or, in some disciplines, a guardian angel or spiritual guide. When all *nine* levels of consciousness are brought into alignment with the *tenth,* the *superconscious* level, enlightenment or the direct experience of truth happens. In all of these ancient systems, the numbers nine and ten are very significant. Nine is the number of the completion of a cycle and ten is a seed number containing both completion and the beginning of a new cycle of creating.

In many of the esoteric disciplines, the path is symbolized by a serpent. The serpent symbolizes the universality of wisdom and the unity of all Creation. The symbol for alchemy is the Hermetic Ouroboros—a serpent with its tail in its mouth. In the Egyptian Mysteries, the serpent path keeps turning back upon itself until the student reaches a ninth and final gate, which leads into the tenth level of Superconscious wisdom.

All the esoteric disciplines lay out some model of a primary path, a Celtic labyrinth or a Tree of Life, which, moving through all the polarities that make up the earthly realms, lead ultimately into universal Truth. All paths lead to God. The numerous correlations within all the ancient mysteries, East or West, indicate that there is a universal Source that created—through diverse spiritual masters in each culture—systems to map the relationship between humanity and God. These esoteric systems give access to the *Reality* of a Divine Universe. They teach how to apply a map that leads to God.

In the Western traditions, the Tree of Life path is believed to be the definitive path, a literal map of the human journey to transmute the heavy-metal density of the earthbound ego as it step-by-step ascends to the pure gold of superconsciousness. The Tree of Life path is believed to represent the path of Divine Spirit on its journey from God to earth. Driven by the creative power of God's Word, Divine Spirit traveled through the ethers, the root substance of all form, creating all the dimensions of consciousness and all manifest earthly life. The student traverses this path—from Malkuth (earth) to Kether (superconsciousness)—over and over, moving with greater and greater consciousness through all the *polarities* that exist in human and earthly consciousness until they reach *unpolarized consciousness*—unity with God.

Each polarity the student passes through and transmutes on the path creates an energy shift that allows the gradual transmutation of ego to essence. As the ego (matter) returns to essence (soul), it becomes more refined and of a pristine gold which the alchemists describe as *not* the gold of the vulgar and greedy. The ego is a piece of work, a piece of consciousness that can't see any piece but its own. We, as alchemists, have undertaken a monumental task, to shift the old world ego into the gold of a new world.

THE ORIGINS OF ALCHEMY

The Hermetic teachings are the source of the science of alchemy. The Hermetic teachings are the work of an ancient Egyptian teacher whom the Greeks named Hermes Trismegistus. Hermes Trismegistus was believed to have been a great spiritual master, so wise that he attained divinity on earth. Legend says Hermes Trismegistus was the teacher of an unknown Egyptian prince who evolved to become the Moses of biblical legend. Hermes was reputed to have lived for over three hundred years and to have been the teacher of Abraham. Some stories propose Hermes and Abraham to have been one and the same. He embodied the qualities of the ancient Greek god Hermes and the Egyptian god Thoth, gods of knowledge, who guided human evolution and were carriers and dispensers of the Word of God. This semi-divine teacher, Hermes Trismegistus, was the author of a spiritual text of great purity, an entirety of truth, universal knowledge which was received directly from the source of all knowledge—from a vast and far-reaching, universal God.

Hermes lives in my heart and my imagination as a master teaching the simplicity of the Word. *Wisdom sings in my soul; my soul sighs for Your Word.* The hieroglyph of the Soul is a living Word. *Behold! Thy soul is a living star!* The Word touches me, touches you. The Word is a living star, a living Light. Bring the Light, the Living

Star, the Vast Fire of God, into the dark, and the power of the Living Light will transmute the dark. This is the simple truth. This is the sacred technology we need.

ALCHEMY

The first known school of alchemy appeared in the city of Alexandria. Alexandria was a consciously created city. Some three hundred years before the death of Christ, Alexander the Great envisioned a great center of learning where the masters of the known world would gather and teach. He created the city of Alexandria and it became the center of Western culture. The Hermetic text, an Arabic and Greek translation of the original Egyptian, was utilized by the scholars and teachers of Alexandria to write the first known alchemical treatise. Alexandria developed a vast university with an international book industry. It became a sanctuary for intellectuals and artists from all over Europe and Asia.

The first century was a time of increased and consolidated power within the emerging Christian and Islamic empires. As their secular power increased, they began to exhibit a brutal intolerance toward esoteric religions. In Alexandria the conflict between the Mystery religions and early Christianity culminated in the brutal death of Hypatia in AD 415. Hypatia was the last great mathematician, alchemist, scholar, and Hermetic teacher in the Alexandrian school. She was pulled from her chariot and torn to pieces by Christian extremists.

Two hundred years later the armies of Islam, responding to an increasingly militant and aggressive Christianity in the Mediterranean world, destroyed much of the library and the book industry in Alexandria. The destruction of Alexandria as a center of Western culture is believed to have helped create the Dark Ages in Europe. After the first century, the Christian Church and the secular state organized to create institutionalized persecutions such as the Inquisition, which sanctified the killing of heretics and witches. The Mystery religions were forced underground.

In the Islamic empire the Mystery religion—the Sufi religion—had a strong influence until the death of the Sufi mystic Al Hallaj. Al Hallaj was crucified for heresy by Islamic religious authorities. He had preached teachings that he claimed had been transmitted from Hermes Trismegistus through a direct lineage of enlightened esoteric teachers, one of whom was Jesus. As the esoteric teachings came under attack in the Mediterranean, the Keepers of the Hermetic Flame fled to England and Italy. They brought with them the essential Hermetic belief that God is a great consciousness, a Mind and a Word, and everything that exists began as cognition, a Living Word from the Mind of God.

The Hermetic teachings thrived in Renaissance Italy and Elizabethan England and along with translations of the Hebrew Kabbalah, created the foundation for the Western Esoteric Tradition. These esoteric mystery teachings have existed like an underground river flowing through history, emerging as underground springs of knowledge in "interesting times" like Renaissance Europe, the late nineteenth century in England and America, and the American 1960s.

THE HERMETIC TEACHINGS

If you study alchemy you are going to run into something referred to as the *Great Work.* The Hermetic teachings conceived of the earth, man, and nature as being characterized by a great *polarity.* The ancient Hermetic masters defined the Great Work of alchemy as the work of utilizing the Fire of God to bring all *polarized* consciousness into one unpolarized or *integrated* consciousness.

Earth is the center of the Great Work. The Hermetic teachings say that Creation will not be complete until humanity accepts its part in Creation, and consciously agrees to the task of creating wisdom on earth. Therefore, human beings are artisans whose work it is to transmute all polarized form into one universal wisdom so that all created form will embody conscious wisdom. Then, as earth is changed from ignorance to wisdom, earth itself becomes the Philosopher's Stone—the Blue Pearl of Wisdom. These Hermetic teachings are the basis for the Western Esoteric Tradition and account for the emphasis on autonomy and personal accountability within that tradition—and for the unpopularity of this system—not everyone is able or ready to deal with that much self-accountability.

"As above, so below" is a Hermetic axiom and the Great Work is to unite the macrocosm (heaven) and the microcosm (earth) in one vessel (the human being) and thus create universal wisdom (Sophia). The principle goal of the Great Work is the *transmutation* of opposites into harmonious wholeness. A basic Hermetic principle is that opposite, contradictory or conflicting poles can unite harmoniously through the transmuting action of a new *Word.* The new Word gives structure to and calls forth an entirely new and beautiful potential from the old form. Trash into treasure. A lump of coal into a diamond. Earthbound lead into heavenly gold.

The Hermetic masters held to their belief that humans have a Divine origin and because they originated from the Word of God are therefore imbued with Divine Spirit. They believed that the superconscious potential for awareness is the faculty through which humans are able to understand and utilize God's Word and consciously participate in the evolution of Earth.

Alchemy begins with the fundamental Hermetic belief that the transmutation of matter into spirit is possible, and not only possible *but the truest desire of Creation!* God's Dream. The Hermetic masters knew that the conscious work of restructuring the polarized energies within matter would create miracles of transmutation on earth *as it is in heaven.* The Hermetic teachings testify to the human capacity to affect the structure of matter by affecting the structure of energy. Matter is structured energy. As above, so below, *matter is structured energy! Matter can be restructured by restructuring energy.*

This revelation, that matter is structured energy, led me beyond intellectual appreciation and into true understanding that matter is first structured in the mind, that a mental creation is an energy template or *thought-form,* and that "form follows thought" is a literal truth. Alchemy is a mental art that creates tangible form in the physical world. This comprehension that polarity is an energy structure as well as a physical structure is a transforming revelation. How does one restructure the energy of a polarity? How can one create an energy powerful enough to transmute the existing energy at an atomic or subatomic level? The ancient Hermeticists began with the knowledge of the *spiritual structure* of existence. They were looking for proof in matter, physical evidence, of the essential spiritual structure of matter. They knew that physical alchemy is only a metaphor for spiritual reality. "As above, so below" is a literal truth that applies to all levels of existence. The ancient Hermeticists believed in and searched for proof in the material world of a great, universal, organizing intelligence that serves as the vital factor in the manifestation of all Creation. Through this vital factor, the transmutation of matter can be accomplished. Therefore, the ancient alchemists, interpreting and utilizing the Hermetic teachings, anticipated the discovery by physicists and mathematicians of the twentieth century of quantum physics, chaos theory, and fractal geometry. The fractal named the Mandelbrot set after the mathematician who *found* it and created fractal geometry, has been called the thumbprint of God.

Mathematics is an amazing language. The Universe is in divine order and mathematics is the language of divine order. Perhaps a fractal is the physical manifestation of Divine Proportion. Divine order, Divine Proportion, equates to "as above, so below". Alchemists knew the thumbprint of God metaphysically as the basic organizing template that acts as a foundation and guide for all created form. The thumbprint of God is a template that exists within every living cell on earth.

I'm not a scientist and some of my interpretations of these fascinating and exciting discoveries might be a bit over the top. It is almost a cliché now that physicists and mathematicians are discovering proof that God's messengers throughout the ages have spoken literal truth. Chaos theory was arrived at through discoveries made by particle physicists. Particle physics, or quantum mechanics, is focused on the subatomic dimension of reality, a world in which waves act like particles and particles act like waves, and there is no way to determine or predict what a particular wave or particle will do. It is impossible to predict the workings of God because you cannot predict all the variables. Chaos theory is a theory that defines a universe in which there is no determinism and the variables appear to be guided by a permeating conscious intention. If everything in creation has an intention that permeates even the minutest sub-atomic particle, then everything in some sense has a life of its own. Therefore, one cannot determine what the universe will do. You can't predict God's thoughts or what makes a wave act like a particle and a particle act like a wave. Prediction is predicated on information that is true and real only in the present moment. A simple choice can change a predicted future. Reality is relative. The determining factor is the Mystery of God.

You could call the Beauty and Mystery of God free will or the existence of choice—or you could call it the existence of a global and cosmic unity consciousness. There is a quantum phenomenon that indicates that subatomic particles, if once associated, remain in contact in a kind of telepathic resonance no matter how far apart they are. If you alter the spin in one particle, its partner immediately alters its spin and matches the change no matter where they are environmentally—water, earth, air, wind, sand, and star—or how distant they are from each other. Science has not determined how or why this happens, just that it does happen. Our ancestors used the same theory when they created sympathetic magic based on the Law of Association and the Law of Contagion—particles of matter, once in intimate energetic, or more specifically, *astral,* contact continue to interact and mirror each other long after the physical contact is broken.

In the Real Magic Course I refer to the existence of variables as creative free-fall, the relationship between the How and the What. The How, the process of Creation, is beautiful and it is orderly as it moves toward bringing the What into existence—but it is an order that cannot be determined by our egocentric consciousness. Perfect order but the process cannot be controlled. *God is uncontrollable but never disorderly!*

There is a wonderful video program of the Mandelbrot set and computer-generated fractals. Seeing it was similar to my first experience of spiritual vision. Like a spiritual vision, the Mandelbrot set is not so much seen as it is experienced. It is evocative. It feels sentient. Speaking a deep mysterious language. Everyone I have shown the fractals video to is reminded of something organic, a sentient form that evokes many forms yet is essentially present as itself. As I watched the video I had flashes of cognition—of a spiritual *Presence*, unmistakable and awesome and at the same time utterly intimate and familiar. The Beauty and Intelligence of God and, simultaneously, home. This experience, in West Africa, would be called the 'flash' of the Spirit. The thumbprint of God.

The Hermetic texts eons ago declared the existence of a universal blueprint, a thumbprint of God, and alchemists, for untold centuries have given their lives to a search for the first manifestation of Divine Spirit, the first manifestation of God's Word. Matter is structured energy. The Word *instructs—imbues energy with intention*—and the intelligence and beauty of God is made tangible. *"In the Beginning was the Word and the Word became Flesh"*. Jesus was the incarnate Word.

THERE ARE NO SECRETS

The Western Esoteric Tradition is a Wisdom tradition, a spirituality formed in the Western world and grounded in natural laws of energy that follow the same creative process whether it be the planting of a seed in the physical earth to produce a plant, or the planting of a seed in consciousness that will produce a new state of being or a new physical form.

The Mystery Schools were not myths. Nor were they occult and hierarchical secret societies. They were universities—institutes of higher learning. The word 'mystery' refers to the ultimate, incomprehensible nature of God. The esoteric masters were guardians of the Hermetic Way, interpreting a philosophy by which a human being could live congruent with the intelligence and beauty of God regardless of religious or cultural beliefs. It is written, *"Know Thyself"*. Self-knowledge is the Great Work. The mystery unfolds within you as you walk the path because there is no end to the mystery of your Self. The Mystery School begins in people with a deep longing for connection with something elemental, beautiful, and real. The Mystery School is, in the words of Jesus, *"seek and ye shall find, knock and it shall be opened, ask and it shall be given."* There are no secrets. There is no secret code to be uncovered only by the righteous and worthy. No one has the center on the Way, the Truth, and the Light. This is a treasure that you uncover from within your Self. The true Mystery School is within you. You are a Keeper of the Flame. You are the Holy Grail.

There has been abuse of esoteric knowledge and frightened people often equate secrecy with power. Some forms of pop occultism are ghastly in their ignorance and superstition. But popular superstition pervades all religion, in the East or in the West, and until all beings are free, fear will create ignorance and ignorance will create superstition and superstition will continue to take awful forms. And to equate gothic romance with alchemy and other esoteric systems is to deny ourselves access to the enormous wisdom to be found in the Western Esoteric Traditions.

Unfortunately, esoteric systems are easily sensationalized in pop culture. The occult attracts many disenfranchised and powerless people who misunderstand and abuse the reputed secrecy in esoteric systems. There is an, "I know a secret and that gives me power over you" aspect to this abuse. Even in the New Age culture there is an aspect of "I know the secrets, I have the center on the secret code" being sold as part of the esoteric spiritual package. Don't buy it. There are no secrets.

There have been historical times of terrible persecution that *required* secrecy and led to a mood of solitude and a desire to stay hidden, on the part of many alchemists. *Because* these ancient systems of alchemy have been abused and often dismissed as occult sensationalism is the best reason to re-present these systems in intelligent and simple ways. *I believe that we, as human beings, carry an inherent gift in our ability to transmute energy. And I believe that learning to use this inherent power is the only technology that human beings need.*

In creating the Real Magic Course I have searched for ways to speak to our present day, accelerated market place world in simple ways that respect all spiritual systems and can cut through the sensationalism, celebrity worship, and self-importance of our time. *Small and simple.* It is *simplicity* that can break the egocentric attraction, the sensational fantasies, and the melodramatic aspects of esoteric teachings and bring them into the simple truth of real magic—the alchemy of self-accountability.

My love and respect for the Hermetic Tradition did not arise because I was looking for privileged information. There is no privileged information. Alchemy simply requires a deep and subtle understanding of energy that anyone can learn. It requires a lot of dedication, rigorous attention and hard work. *Simple but not easy.* The alleged secrecy around alchemy arises from the fact that the principles are simple, subtle, and *literal.* Such simple and subtle truth carries its own protection from abuse. The type of secrecy that promotes elitism and separatism has no place within systems like the Hermetic teachings, which exist in the openness of the Christ Consciousness. When there is such openness all contradictions are resolved. When there is no more search, no such thing as a correct answer, one is forced to let go of manipulation (such as secrecy) and simply be true.

There are no secrets. There is no new knowledge. Knowledge of the Hermetic teachings opens a Way to the re-translation and utilization of ancient, existing knowledge. The Holy Grail is the grail of self-knowledge—that is the big secret. The Holy Grail is not outside the Self; the Self *is* the Holy Grail. The integral human being is the divine and perfect chalice. Cherish ourselves; cherish each other. There is nothing new under the sun. Whatever mistaken beliefs and superstitions have been imposed on alchemy, whatever your point of view; *alchemy is about liberation*—the gold of consciousness freed after being trapped for lifetimes in the heavy metal density of unconscious ego.

The alchemist searches for self-knowledge. In the reality of this search, all so-called secrets are revealed as 'no-secret'. When every path has been walked, every obstacle transmuted, every dream of material treasure revealed to be ephemeral, to be illusion; when one arrives at the center of the labyrinth, one finds nothing. No Thing. Silence. No concepts, no tasks, no Grail. Only the simple truth. Only the Beauty of God.

The search for God, the Sacred Matrix, the Holy Grail, the Great Work, is a search for Self that has moved humanity for centuries out of the swamp of ego and toward the Light of Spirit. This is the faith we keep. We are all alchemists. This is our agreement with God. And as we move through all the polarities, all the dimensions of consciousness that make up the realms of human reality, we move finally into the realm of the Superconscious and through this Christ Consciousness we meet God's Dream. One Light.

It was there all the time. It has always been there. There was nothing to search for.

The ancient Egyptians declared that the Soul is a living Star, a spark from the Fire of God. The Sufi teacher Rumi declares, as do so many teachers, the existence of One Light—shining through many lamps. Same thing. No matter how different the lamps are, the Light is the same. Whatever path you choose to follow, your true teacher is your own living star and you are an artisan on a creative mission to make your life a thing of beauty, wisdom, and simple happiness. And as you work through all the polarities that interfere with that simple knowing, you leave a path of Light to guide the world.

PART TWO

THE REAL MAGIC COURSE

Alchemy is the Art
Of taking your trash—
And turning it into Treasure.

CHAPTER 1

THE GREAT WORK

True Hermetic Transmutation is a Mental Art. If the Universe is Mental in its nature, then Mental Transmutation must be the Art of Changing the Conditions of the Universe, along the lines of Matter, Force, and Mind. So you see, therefore, that Mental Transformation is really the "magic" of which the ancient writers had so much to say in their mystical works and about which they gave so few practical instructions.

The Kybalion

THE REAL MAGIC Course incorporates the Hermetic "Mental Art" in a way that allows us in this age of technology to use the practical instructions that are obscured in the ancient teachings. Using these teachings in practical, daily ways, allows us to create a way of life that is beautiful in the way any work of art is beautiful. A work of art is eloquent and coherent and true, and the creation of it requires self-inquiry, hard work, struggle, commitment, patience, devotion and dedication. In return it is utterly rewarding and makes you, no matter the circumstances, completely happy. The Real Magic Course is my work of art. There is nothing new in the Course, it restructures basic philosophies and principles of the Hermetic teachings to create a spiritual path for today's world. I call it *real magic* because it is authentic and can help you to create authentic change.

What is magic? Magic is a sacred technology. Magic is the Beauty and Intelligence of God in action. Magic in its workings has a lucid intelligence that is more akin to higher physics than it is to popular occult and psychological interpretations of what magic is. Magic is a creative and sacred art. That is why magic is often difficult to define or interpret. The Tao of magic is like a labyrinth that is new and evocative each time the path is walked. No one can predict how a sacred path will evolve. The Tao of the Real Magic Course creates a sacred existence for each person who walks the path.

Magic is about energy. Magic informs us that everything is energy and energy does things; energy makes things happen. Magic is like jazz; it is improvised from a highly creative, deeply and intelligently structured knowledge that can't be known or experienced intellectually. It has to be lived. And, like jazz, if you don't live it, it won't come out your horn. There is no difference between creating a piece of music, a painting, poem, or sculpture and creating magic. Magic utilizes energy in ways that transmute existing reality. An artist utilizes energy in ways that transmute existing reality. In the Real Magic Course you learn to use the sacred Hermetic technology to create a life that is your work of art.

Hermetic Alchemy has always dealt with the mastery of Mental Forces rather than material elements. The transmutation of one quality of vibration into another. This statement from *The Kybalion* sums up the difference between the alchemy of the Middle Ages which dealt with physical elements, and the ancient Egyptian Hermetic teachings which focused on the transmutation of one state of consciousness to another. The Real Magic Course is about consciousness. It is not about tools and rituals; it is about the energy that makes both the tools and the inspiration to use them, possible. I use no rituals and no shamanistic ceremonies in the Course. No drumming, no feathers, symbols, candles, chanting, or incense. Magic is a technology of consciousness wherein consciousness itself is the tool used to create the changes in consciousness that are required before a new form can come into being.

Everything in the universe is energetically connected; energy creates patterns and patterns give structure to energy. It is true that consciousness shapes reality, and it is also true that reality shapes consciousness. There is no separation. No rituals or ceremonies are needed in the reality of consciousness. No rituals are needed in the reality of transmutation. The only tool required is your mind and your willingness to expand your horizons.

Utilizing a sacred technology requires learning a new and different kind of thought process, a specific way of looking at words that is a departure from our prevailing linear way of thinking. The thought process of magic begins with duality, transmutes the duality, and arrives at integration. The highest frequency of heavenly truth begins on earth, where the Fire of God incorporates and transforms the lowest frequency of false truth. "As above, so below" means there is no separation between the One Source and the many. No separation is both the truth about life and a Hermetic spiritual ideal to strive for. *Transformation doesn't begin in the spiritual ideals no matter how well you intellectually comprehend them.* Transformation begins in the polarity—the space between your deepest fears and your greatest potential. To transmute energy you have to begin with where you are at, with the contradictions, the confusion, and pain that characterizes a polarized consciousness. In the Course you begin a path toward truth right in the middle of your most painful contradictions.

I first truly understood what the Course was—or what the Course wanted to be as it always had a life of its own—on a trip to West Africa in 1986. On this trip I "saw" the difference between transference and direct transformation. It was a revelation that changed my approach to life. When I say that I "saw", I mean it literally. All my life I have been a seer. I love that old-fashioned word and use it deliberately. When I finally, in my late thirties, began accepting who I am rather than cursing the God from which I came, I accepted that word "seer" as it applied to myself. I see energetically. And more than that, I *comprehend* energetically. I understand *what* energy is doing and *why* it is doing what it is doing. Seeing is *comprehension,* the mind in the flesh, the Flash of Spirit.

On this trip to Togo, West Africa, I observed a shaman do a series of healings. Energetically, I could see that he was *transferring* the energy of the disease from the patient to the animals that he used in the ceremony. He used chickens and ducks and in one extreme case a goat. After he had transferred the energy of the disease to the animal, his assistant would ceremoniously butcher the animal. As the animal died the thought-form energy of the disease would dissipate—it would "die". This is not a psycho-mental metaphor; it is a literal, energetic fact that I observed time after time with more than one healer.

I observed this shaman for three days, amazed by his intelligence, his dedication to his people, his knowledge of herbs and healing and the sheer power of his beliefs. At the end of three days, while meditating beside the Atlantic Ocean, I had a revelation about the difference between *transference* and direct *transformation.* Transference is an old shamanistic belief and an archaic way of working with energy. In direct transformation, the energy of the disease is transmuted without a go-between, and it ceases to exist energetically—i.e., it no longer exists as a thought form. A medium is not required to create that transformation. Direct transformation is a d*irect transmutation* of an existing energy. The energy does not first need to be transferred to a physical object before it can be transmuted. At that moment, I determined that I *would* understand alchemy and teach it according to this revelation. I *knew* that I would create some style of a mystery school course and teach people that they could directly, without the use of a medium, transmute the energy of their fear and pain.

Until that moment I had been playing tug-of-war with God. I had been teaching for years but reluctantly—I didn't want to be a spiritual or New Age teacher. I was stubbornly maintaining my autonomy and privacy, my identity as an artist and a mother. As I sat meditating on that African beach, I clearly heard the words "As above, so below," as if Hermes was speaking directly to me. I understood at that moment that the next step in the evolution of the species is that we learn the difference between *transference* and direct transformation. At this moment of realization I felt that my commitment to teaching was crucial.

This is the Great Work. Human beings are God's alchemists. We can create beautiful work-of-art lives and live them on the most beautiful planet in the Universe. At the time, contemplating the path I was about to walk and the reality of the commitment I was making, I felt very isolated. I felt more like God's fool than like God's alchemist but I have always loved God foolishly.

It is hard work, learning the Great Work. Learning to *think in a new way* requires a restructuring of the way we process ideas and the way that we relate to problems. The training involved in restructuring your thought process requires you to use your *attention* in new and conscious ways that pull your brain into confusion and discomfort—and your discomfort doesn't stop until confusion becomes clarity and you embark on a great love affair with life. Your fear is transmuted to faith. You emerge in love. In love with God, in love with the life within you and in love with all beings. And in a true, non-idealistic way, in love with Reality. Learning to think in a new way teaches you to *be* in a new way.

It is very important in this process toward freedom to *not* make spiritual practices complicated. They are difficult and rigorous and this needs to be accepted. There is no such thing as a spiritual "fix". No instant gratification. Often in today's new spiritual culture you meet with the expectation that spiritual change is easy, that when you commit to a spiritual path life becomes mellow; you bliss out and have no more problems. This is a misunderstanding. Transformation is simple but rigorous.

The practice of Real Magic requires that you not lie to yourself about or deny the state of the world or the state of your immediate, present life. Unconditional love is not idealistic. We must not idealize suffering, or glorify victims. Human beings are creative beings living in a suffering world. We never stop receiving challenges to our creativity and we never stop creating, never stop using our ability to heal, our ability to transmute energy.

Transformation is a spiritually creative process that is not scary or life threatening but it can feel that way. When you embark on a path of transformation, your ego-centered beliefs are challenged in simple ways that can't be understood or explained psychologically or intellectually. Your ego loses all its safe places when you step into Light but once you directly experience Light, you feel safe for the first time in your life. Achieving the simple spiritual experience of faith requires dedication, lots of attention, hours of practice, and hard work. A spiritual path requires a commitment to your own intelligent promise as a human being.

It takes rigorous attention to change centuries-old habits and beliefs. This is what you undertake when you begin a path of transformation. As you walk the path you learn a sense of wonder and self-respect that comes from utilizing resources you didn't know you had, resources that awaken within you as you walk the path. Such a Creative Way of life teaches you the wise use of energy. Utilizing these creative spiritual tools will help you make your life an expression of your Soul's truth. You are here to be a gesture from your Soul; every thought, every movement, an expression of the Beauty of your Self. You are the Great Work and you are here to live your real life. When you commit your heart and soul to doing the Great Work you learn the power and grace that comes from living a conscious life and serving the evolution of conscious life on earth.

CHAPTER 2

CREATING TRASH OR TREASURE?—SOME AGREEMENTS

THIS IS A beautiful planet. Why is it that human beings seem unable to live in this world in a state of gratitude and beauty? The human condition of marginal life, of lack, ignorance and fear seems to be escalating. Does this escalating state of lack, ignorance, fear and conflict signify the end of civilization as we know it? Or will we now take this chance we are being given and create a world of beauty, health, and wise nurturing for all beings? How do we create the kind of changes we need to create if the world is going to be a world of authentic unity and grace?

Perhaps the answer lies in our relationship with problems. Krishnamurti has stated over and over again that the way that you approach a problem is more important than the actual problem. The Hermetic teachings have given the world an approach to problems that is focused on the transformation of dualities. We live in a world where the transcendence or transformation of duality is called a miracle and is considered the province of God. If we use the Hermetic approach, we can look at duality not as opposing intentions as in good and evil, but as a polarity that contains a hidden potential, the diamond in the lump of coal. If we embrace contradiction as a polarized creative energy, a tension that can release the Beauty of God, we can create our own miracles and the greatest miracle of all—an unpolarized consciousness. If Jesus was a glorious impossibility then we all have it in us to achieve the impossible. That means we have to think in terms of the impossible. We are programmed to think in terms of only what is possible. We are taught that any other kind of thinking is for airheads. We aren't taught to air dream, to think in terms of allowing the impossible to manifest. When the impossible appears in our life we fear it and try to fit it into the shape of what we know is possible. And of course, it doesn't fit. So we call it occult or contradictory and we fear.

In the Course practices, we consciously utilize the impossible; we make use of the energy of contradiction; we utilize the energy of polarity to arrive at unpolarized consciousness or nonduality. From within our polarized self, we can release an integrated, transcendent Self, a consciousness that is in constant, simple, agreement with the Reality of God. The Reality of God is a Dream, both the Fire and the Water of Life, a vast intelligence, an all-inclusive, all-creative Consciousness that is characterized by an all-pervading unconditional Love. If human consciousness is a spark from that Fire, what can we not do if we live our lives congruent with the Beauty and Intelligence of God's Dream?

Perhaps only God and the earth can take a literal lump of coal and turn it into a literal diamond, but you can learn to take the vibration of your pain and fear, your self-condemnation, your failure, any quality of life that you are defining as hopeless, your metaphoric lumps of coal and transmute them into the opposite polarity—diamonds. And once your lump of coal is transmuted it no longer exists; once you've turned your trash into treasure, your trash is gone. Or, at least, it can and should be.

Unfortunately, human beings will often at the first sign of treasure, turn it into trash. I call this the mystery of the human ego. The Mystery of God can change trash into treasure, coal into diamond, but only the human ego is perverse enough to turn a potential diamond into a lump of coal or potential treasure into trash.

Real Magic's basic premise: an unconscious process of creating trash can be turned into a conscious process of creating treasure. Human beings are equally good at creating trash or creating treasure. Why? Because human beings are creative beings and human beings are good at transmuting energy. Trash or treasure, it is all the same process. But we don't know that. No one tells us. No one tells us that the reason we are good at turning our potential diamonds into lumps of coal is because we are good at transmuting energy. It is our ability to transmute energy combined with our ability to manifest new forms that makes us good at sabotaging ourselves. Did anyone tell you that the first time you sabotaged yourself? Did they tell you that you could easily reverse the process and turn self-sabotage into success? No. No one tells us that. So we easily and all unknowingly learn to sabotage our treasure because we don't know one simple fact—we are alchemists. God meant us to be. We *are* energy and we know everything we need to know about being energy and transmuting energy and creating glorious impossibilities.

You can create changes that are so real that your old existence doesn't ever again come back as a crippling remembrance of past guilt or pain. The past is not supposed to haunt and cripple us. It is supposed to teach us who we are and what we truly want. It is supposed to move us to create, to raise pain into inspiration and inspiration into wisdom, to raise fear into compassion. This is the challenge of the past. Often the past teaches by teaching us about adversity and what it is like to live a marginal existence, to feel powerless and afraid. No one should have to, in any circumstance, live powerless and afraid. No human being should have to accept that violence is an unchangeable human condition. This is wrong. It is a rip-off of our birthright as creative beings born into a creative universe. Don't accept it. Do not allow that belief to reincarnate in you—allow it to dissipate.

We could live on this planet as if each day we awaken in our Mothers' garden, new and renewed, living in peace and beauty. For the sake of all beings, choose to master the art of taking your trash and turning it into Treasure.

YOUR REALITY

I begin the Course by asking you to make some agreements about your world. Your world. No one else's. No two snowflakes are alike. No two human beings are alike. No two worlds are alike. You can't live in someone else's world. You can't live in what someone else has created. You cannot change another person's world. You live in your world. You can change your world; you can transmute energy and change your reality. The New Age truism, "You Create Your Own Reality" actually is true and refers to your own personal reality. This does not mean you are to blame for every bad thing that happens in the world. It means your personal world—no one else's. Taking charge of your personal creations requires that you practice self-awareness and the conscious use of your attention. And it is necessary to take a look at the word "responsibility" as representing your response to your environment. Your environment is always throwing challenges your way. You have a choice about responding from a victim mentality or responding from a desire to manifest truth. Responsibility does not mean blame. It simply means that you choose how you are going to respond. So you might as well begin with some agreements to let go of the word "blame" and pick up the word "responsibility". Agree to stop blaming yourself, stop blaming others, and stop looking for who to blame when something upsetting happens. This does not mean that you cultivate a greedy or selfish point of view in the guise of creating your vision. It means that you agree to create the world you truly choose to live in by choosing to make a conscious response to challenges, you choose to pay attention to what you bring into being in your world. It means self-inquiry and self-accountability and, ultimately, self-knowledge.

You cannot make choices for another person. You are not responsible for other people's choices and for what other people create. You cannot easily change the basic and collective human beliefs that create the world. But you can take responsibility for your own creative nature and change your inner world to the point where your life orientation is one of faith, trust, strength, and real knowledge, where the choices you make come from knowledge of who you are and have real power in your real world. This change within you changes the outer world. So make an agreement that you will practice no more blame—and especially you will practice no more self-condemnation. And agree that you will practice being aware of the choices you make and aware of what manifests in your life from the choices you make. Don't focus on other people's choices; that is a distraction. Focus on your own choices but with no self-condemnation when your choices seem to be wrong or when life seems to go wrong.

I ask you to make an agreement about the nature of reality. That which we call "reality" is a giant tapestry, an energy weave of interwoven beliefs, choices, and creations. In this energy weave, nothing is absolute. The weave is always changing. You create your own piece of that weave from your beliefs, expectations, attitudes, desires, fears, judgments, definitions, interpretations, assumptions, feelings, intentions—through your most consistent and persistent thoughts. Any change in your weave changes the whole grid system. If you restructure your thoughts and create a new thought process, a new approach to problems, your reality changes. Your piece of the weave changes. Authentic inner change creates authentic outer change. "As above, so below" is a Hermetic axiom. Create another: "as within, so without". What you carry within creates your personal world. You create your world, and you carry it with you wherever you go. This is why changing jobs or changing locations doesn't always make you happier or more successful or more fulfilled. Agree that your world will now be a masterpiece of harmony and beauty and commit yourself to the creation of that world.

BELIEF AND FREEDOM

What is Freedom? Freedom means to live with no resistance, with no "yes, but . . ." and no "if only . . ." If you live in a state of resistance, there is no freedom. What is our greatest obstacle to freedom? Belief. The very nature of belief sets up a state of resistance. Beliefs carry with them a commitment to guard, protect and defend the belief. In this way beliefs promote separation. The belief that separatism is a desirable state is our greatest obstacle to freedom.

Freedom is a state of being that does not have to be defended or proved. It stands as it is. It is freedom. If freedom is a state that cannot be defined, then we must look at what is not freedom in order to examine freedom. We must look at belief—the true nature of belief.

What is belief? There is a myth among academic anthropologists that it is belief that creates magic, that the reason magic was powerful to our ancestors was because everyone in the tribe or village believed in it. This implies that you have to believe in magic before you can practice and create magic. Not so. Magic is about energy, about what energy does. Magic is what happens when you set up the conditions that create a transmutation of energy. Belief is a powerful force in the world. Beliefs create tremendous amounts of energy, but belief is not required in order to transmute energy. Why? Because it is not belief that transmutes energy. Energy transmutes energy. The reason beliefs seem powerful is that they contain tremendous amounts of fixed energy. Fixed energy is fixed attention, attention that has been glued in place. Because beliefs contain the energy of fixed attention, it takes a tremendous amount of energy to shift a belief. The shift in the energy of belief creates change. Therefore, belief does not create change. Energy creates change. Energy does things. Energy makes things happen. The necessary energy can come from a belief, or it can come from conscious spiritual practices. Belief is not required. Energy is required.

Like my anthropologist friend says, "Your version of magic is too simple to be believed." Don't waste your time trying to believe or disbelieve any of this. It is not necessary to believe the Hermetic principles; it is only necessary to practice them. The Course practices teach you to create, hold, and focus tremendous amounts of energy. If you practice these spiritual practices, you will create tremendous amounts of focused energy. Energy creates change. Energy makes things happen. Energy does things. Repeat that over and over until it takes. Believe that.

What is belief? Belief is an idea or experience that has been incorporated into your identity as a deep emotional certainty about life. Beliefs come from your own experience, from the conclusions you have made about life. They also come from ideas passed down from parents, teachers, and religious and cultural authorities. Beliefs create your view of your world. Beliefs tell you what is true and real in your world, and therefore, your belief systems create the conditions and expectations that color your relationship with reality.

The nature and purpose of belief is to maintain an unchanging human identity. This is the province of the human ego. The nature of belief is not bad. The bad, or negative, aspect of belief is in the human egoistic tendency to cling to beliefs that already exist and to resist or ignore new information that might be truer and more supportive of life than the existing belief. It is almost a cliché now that beliefs can cause violence and promote separation and conflict between peoples, but the source of conflict is in attachment—clinging to beliefs as if they are absolute truth—and believing that your world will not be safe until you enlist everyone you know in your beliefs. A world of beliefs at war with other beliefs has created a world of war, a world that believes in and relies on violence to solve problems.

Beliefs lead to many conditions. A condition is anything that you believe has to happen before you can accept something else. For example, "Prove that you love me, and I will love you back". "I won't be all right unless such and such happens—unless I am loved or unless I get rich". "Prove that I can trust you and then I will trust you". Prove it. Conditions are insatiable; there is always a new condition that must be met before one can feel safe. To live conditionally is to live provisionally and marginally. A condition imposes on, changes, or restricts the nature of the thing in question. In order for your beliefs to be validated, "others" must meet your conditions. You have a large emotional investment here.

Conditions lead to expectations. Expectations are always about outcomes—what must happen, what is owed to you or necessary for the survival of your identity. And for your identity to survive within the reality you inhabit, your reality must not change. This means that control is necessary for your survival—it is imperative that you control all incoming information, and that you control the outcomes in your environment. This is a primary condition. Your outcome thinking fits itself to your beliefs. This is serious.

Anyone who doesn't meet your conditions and fulfill your great expectations threatens your survival. This is very primal energy. It is not surprising that beliefs can create violent reaction—rage—and are so often fought over, attacked or defended to the death. Inherent in the notion of belief is the belief that you cannot be truly safe unless everyone in your environment subscribes to the same belief system. That sounds a little crazy on a planet of diversity where there are as many beliefs as there are human beings. Perhaps we need to create a planetary consciousness that doesn't need beliefs, that lives by faith and a nurturing love for and celebration of life.

The most difficult belief to transcend is the bone-deep, primal human belief that we live in a dangerous world filled with potentially dangerous others and all those potentially dangerous others must be converted or destroyed. This is what keeps sinking our attempts to create peace. Until this fundamental belief is transmuted it will undermine human sanity, for we will keep creating evidence to back up the belief.

If you make an agreement to practice the art of deliberate choice, to practice not taking beliefs personally, to not be afraid to be wrong, to leave a space around you of openness and willingness to change, you establish a powerful step toward freedom. And you must continually make this agreement because your ego is protecting your old world, it protects your personal version of reality, and you have a serious emotional investment in keeping your world intact. This creates problems when you try to make changes. Make an agreement with your self to let your beliefs stand as they are. Look at them as bundles of energy you are carrying that represent conclusions you have come to about life and agree to keep your mind and heart open to new experiences, new knowledge, and new conclusions. Be willing to let go of the bundles that might be inhibiting your freedom. Be willing to receive and carry new bundles of faith, of patience, kindness, and compassion.

The choice to address belief directly must be strong and constant. Human beings are trained to worship belief, to view our beliefs as realities that we will, if necessary, fight and die for. Human beliefs about patriotism, tribe, race, and religion, are deep emotional systems that can be handed down in families, in tribes, in countries, for generations. Human beings are deeply imprinted with human beliefs about ownership as safety. We believe that exclusive ownership and separation will keep us safe. We do not so much believe our beliefs as possess them. Mine. My country, my tribe, my children, right or wrong—mine.

Practice looking at beliefs not as intense, do or die for emotional investments, but as unconscious choices you've made and incorporated into yourself, often from secondhand and outdated information and from other people's experience. Tell yourself that a belief is simply information that you have decided is true. Tell yourself that it is all right to change your mind if new information that proves to be true is experienced. Looking at your beliefs as choices you can make or unmake gives you the freedom to create tremendous amounts of energy. It takes tremendous amounts of energy to transmute the energy of fixed beliefs. Agree to pay attention to your choices, and rather than relying on choices you have made in the past that come from old beliefs and assumptions, be willing to make new choices and learn from the new choices. Be willing to trust that the action of making deliberate choices is bringing you closer to your true existence.

Once you experience being true to yourself and realize that belief is not required for safety or happiness, you open to the experience of faith. Faith is very different from belief. Faith cannot be described but it is unmistakable once it manifests within you. The difference between faith and belief has to do with accountability and in a system like the Hermetic esoteric system, which requires deep self-inquiry, personal accountability is a necessary requirement. Faith comes from trust. Self-inquiry and a willingness to be accountable to one's Self and accountable to an even greater Truth than we can know, creates a deep and abiding trust in our choices. Faith is born when we choose to honor and trust and learn from our own choices. Faith teaches us that there is more to life than we can understand and that in order to honor and nourish the growth of wisdom, we must be willing to be accountable to others and to ourselves and to that greater Source of wisdom and beauty that we call God. Faith comes gently and subtly and is free from attachment. Because of its deeply gentle nature and its serenity, faith does not have to be defended. It arises from our own true spiritual experience; it comes from knowing rather than belief, and it has no quarrel with any aspect of God. Faith enhances rather than conflicts with your chosen way of life. Faith can enhance your beliefs but will not lead to violent reaction if your beliefs are questioned because faith does not carry the same compulsion to prove itself as belief does.

POWER

There are many clichés about power—power corrupts, power leads to power struggles, power can be abused, and these clichés are more about fear than they are about power. Power in itself is not a necessarily a bad thing. It is not power that is abused. Authority is abused. Having a position of authority can tempt someone who feels powerless to exercise that authority in unfair and even damaging ways. But being in a position of authority does not necessarily mean that a person is powerful. Power has to do with energy—the amount of energy you have, or the amount you can raise and hold in your consciousness. Power has to do with focused consciousness, focused attention, focused intention. Power has to do with being true to yourself, being an integrated self. If you are true to your own integrity, with no fear and no attachment, you no longer give anyone or anything authority over you. In this case, you are not likely to abuse the authority given to you because it will be authentic. Powerless is an illusion fostered by those who abuse authority in order to manipulate and hoard other people's energy.

Why is it important for you to claim your power? Power means no one and nothing can make you do or say or be something that is not true to you. Power means you no longer give anyone the power to affect your choices, or affect your feelings about yourself. You never again violate your own integrity because of fear of consequences. Power means never again believing you have to lie, or make excuses for your choices, or explain yourself to authority figures. Power means you never again believe you have to manipulate truth in order to make the significant others in your life happy. Power is knowing that happiness, that truth itself, cannot exist if it is founded on illusion, denial, or on bearing false witness against yourself or any other being. Power is knowing that there is no difference between a little white lie and full-out fraud. Power is available to everyone. That is why it is important for you to claim your power.

The power of being true to yourself comes as you transmute the energy of destructive emotions into the energy of qualities—like patience, strength, faith, wisdom, truth, fearlessness, compassion—that you choose to bring into being and embody in yourself. And this cannot be done intellectually or mentally. It must be done by transmuting the energy of the destructive feeling. You must choose the qualities you most want to embody in spite of any contradictory or destructive feelings you might be feeling. It doesn't matter how you feel. The feeling of the moment does not matter—that feeling comes from the past, is about the past, and is a product of past beliefs. So you cannot look at the feeling of the moment as a guide for the reality of the moment. The quality you most want to embody, in reality, right now, is what matters—this quality is about the moment. This quality embodies what you would most like to bring to life in yourself. This quality is a vital part of your work of art.

Emotions are powerful and produce strong feelings. Don't give power to your feelings. Your spiritual practices might not match your feelings, might bring up feelings of resistance, fear, or resentment, and in this case, your feelings are not the important factor. This work is not therapy. This is alchemy, the science of transmuting energy. On one hand, you have a spiritual practice; on the other hand you have your feelings. Which is more important, your creative spiritual adventure, your integrated Self, or your doubt, mistrust, suspicion, anger, self-pity, fear—all your symptoms of self-importance? These feelings that arise from your old destructive reality and your old beliefs about who you are, *are not truth.* They are old stories that keep you in a constant melodramatic approach to conflict. Feelings give you clues about what it is you want to transmute. Your feelings are not who you are.

In the Hawaiian Kahuna tradition, emotions and feelings are looked at as an indication that a belief system has been energized. Emotions and feelings are not to be projected or repressed; they are to be examined for clues about yourself. They are opportunities for greater self-knowledge. The moment you feel the emotion is the moment of opportunity, the moment to make a choice about transmuting the emotion. When overwhelmed by emotion, don't suppress the emotion, acknowledge it but cultivate the practice of saying to yourself that it is not the emotion that is important, it is the quality you want to manifest in that moment that is important. The transmutation of the emotion is important.

You are always powerful. This has been said so often in the New Age culture that it has become a cliché. Another saying that has become a cliché is that you can only receive what you have agreed to have. I don't ask you to mindlessly go around saying, "I am always powerful." I ask you to agree to receive power and to deliberately pretend that you have the power, in each and every moment, to transmute your destructive beliefs and the feelings they create. Deliberately pretend. Conjure. Call into being the power to transmute the destructive emotions.

Deliberately pretending you have something you can not actually believe you have is a powerful agreement. This is not fantasy, or denial, or any form of lying. Deliberation is not the same as fantasy. Fantasy is almost always compensation for something you believe you lack and it always centers on an emotional attachment and a belief that you are powerless to manifest what you want. Deliberation is a focused attention that does not require an emotional investment. The Sufi teacher Rumi, in a poem about deliberation, said deliberation means to sniff with your wisdom nose before swallowing an offering. Deliberation is two-headed and happens when you become at ease with contradictions. You can observe with one head and see clearly where you are at, at what is, even if it is painful. Then with your other head, you can look ahead to the existence you truly want, choose to receive that new existence, and with deliberation, act as if your new existence already exists at some level of possibility. This requires the ability to focus your attention. It requires a clear intention and a clear choice. It requires conscious faith. It requires you to be at ease with contradictions. Being at ease with contradictions is a powerful state of being. It is a state of trust. Make an agreement to be at ease with the contradiction between who you believe you are and who you actually are.

What does being a two-headed person, at ease with contradictions, mean? It means you are never in bondage to anything you have ever heard, read or believed to be true. This state of creative self-knowledge is available to you. Truth is always available to you. All human beings are creative beings. Agree that as a creative being, you are always powerful. You are not in bondage to your own or anyone else's beliefs, perceptions, and predictions about the past and future. Attachment is bondage. Not being attached to fixing contradictions, not being attached to particular outcomes, being truth orientated and not outcome orientated, and not being attached to taking everything personally, gives you the power to shift energies in the moment in ways that will transmute the energy of your old existence. This is power.

CHAPTER 3

THE ALCHEMY OF MANIFESTING: AN OVERVIEW OF THE COURSE

All paradoxes may be reconciled

The Kybalion

"THE ALCHEMY OF *Manifesting*" serves as the Course textbook. To create this overview for the book I have expanded on the original text that I use in the Course. This chapter will assist my students or anyone who wishes to create study groups. In the chapters to come I take a deeper look at some of the concepts mentioned in this overview.

THE ALCHEMY OF MANIFESTING

You are going to create a masterpiece. Your masterpiece begins with your problems, your fears, with the lumps of coal in your life that you are most anxious about. You are going to approach these present obstacles and potential treasures in a magical way that will manifest a world of beauty and Truth.

What is manifesting? Manifesting is the process of using universal laws of energy to transmute one state of existence to another state of existence. This is a natural process that is present unconsciously in all human beings—people do it all the time. The Real Magic Course teaches you to apply this process in a *conscious* way and *consciously* change your existence.

Manifesting in alchemical terms is the process of releasing the potential form that exists within polarity. For example, fear contains the potential for fearless. Anxiety contains the potential for serenity. Illness contains the potential for health. Lead contains the potential for gold. Coal contains the potential for diamond. This is literal potential, not metaphoric potential—the real thing, not a model of the thing or an idea about the thing. What is fear giving you? What is your problem giving you? *The opportunity to create a new existence.* The opportunity to approach problems in a new way; the Hermetic way.

The Hermetic approach to problems is to consciously polarize the problem. The principle of polarity is the most important of the Hermetic formula. It gives us an approach to problems that takes the problem out of the realm of conflict and stress and into the realm of Creation.

Polarity. What do I mean by that?

In Real Magic I use the principle of polarity to create a visible map of two relatively "true" but opposite poles. I call it a visible map because you actually write it down as side A and side B. Side A is a visible word map of your stress, which leads you to side B as a visible word map of your possible fulfillment.

When you have something in your life that is stressful or problematic you have one part of a polarity. The energy of stress is locked into one particular side of the polarity. Call the stress side of the polarity side A. Your first objective is to release the energy of creative potential that is locked up in this one-sided polarity. To release this potential energy, you must seek out the other side of the polarity, the opposite pole. Call the opposite pole side B. Each of these poles contains a story about reality. One reality exists in your life; the other reality is yet to be born. *Both are true.* Opposite poles contain tremendous amounts of creative potential. In order to release one pole of reality and bring into being the opposite pole, you need energy. Opposite poles have magnetism and this magnetic attraction can attract and hold *tremendous* amounts of energy.

Tremendous amounts of energy are necessary because it is energy that *makes things happen.* So your first thought might be how do you create the energy? How does the earth take a lump of coal and turn it into a diamond? *Heat.* In alchemy, energy is a metaphor for heat. You have the capacity to, using the power of your attention, create an energy that is equivalent to tremendous heat and use it to manifest change. Imagine that as an alchemist of consciousness, you are working with the Secret of Fire. The Secret of Fire is in the fuel. *Fire transmutes the fuel.* The problem you are stressing about is the fuel. A conscious polarity gives you a map of where you want to focus the energy of letting go of stress, and it shows you where to focus the energy (heat) that will transmute the stress (fuel). Utilizing the principle of polarity to create a visible map helps you create and hold energy. It also shows the energy where to go and shows it what to do. So you could also call side A "fuel" and side B "transmuter".

This is the basic premise of alchemy—in order to transmute energy you need to *consciously* create a greater intensity of energy than the energy that already exists in the form you want to transmute. How do you create the energy/heat that will take your stress and turn it into treasure? Two things. One, you must learn to *focus* your attention. Focused attention concentrates energy and creates metaphoric heat. Two, you must also have a strong intention. Intention *instructs and directs* the energy. Using the principle of polarity and the power of your attention and intention in a conscious way gives you the ability to create tremendous amounts of energy and direct that energy toward the intention you most want to bring into being.

How do you do that? Where do you begin?

You start with where you are at—start with your problem, your anxiety, your stress, your trash, your lump of coal. This is your fuel. Use your mind, your attention, your longing for change, and your willingness to receive a new existence, to build a fire that will transform your fuel. Your stress is your departure point for arriving at serenity. Your trash is the beginning of your treasure. Your lump of coal is the beginning of your diamond. The first thing you do in order to create and move tremendous amounts of energy is to start right where you are and create your conscious polarity. Using the principle of polarity, you create a polarity map. You "name" your problem the point of *departure*, and call it Point A. Then you follow a line to the opposite pole and you name it the point of your *arrival* and you call it Point B. Clear opposite poles give you a departure point and a place to arrive. Not a place to stop. Creation never stops. *A place to arrive.* A place to realize fulfillment. Realized fulfillment is what every human being wants. As you arrive at a point of fulfillment, the receiving itself teaches you and moves you to your next fulfillment. What is fulfillment? You are hungry. You fix a meal and you eat it. This is realized fulfillment, a fulfillment that is unmistakable and that you easily receive. Manifesting should be as easy as saying, "I'm hungry, please pass the broccoli and yams."

Anything in your life that causes you stress, anxiety, or unhappiness, anything you would like to change can be made into a polarity. Always start with Point A. Point A is a tangible reality in your life. It might be invisible but you are experiencing it in a definite, tangible way. For example, fear is invisible, but what manifests from your fear is a tangible reality.

* * *

> *To destroy an undesirable rate of mental vibration, put in operation the Principle of Polarity and concentrate upon the opposite pole to that which you desire to suppress. Kill out the undesirable by changing its Polarity.* (*The Kybalion)*

If you have two extremes of the same thing—like hate and love—you have two poles that express varying degrees *of the same line*. These extremes can meet in a *new existence* that is more powerful than each of the poles. It is possible to change the energy of one pole to the other pole by changing *the vibration of the line*. It is possible to transmute the vibration of fear (point A) into the vibration of fearless (point B) by polarizing along the line and focusing in the direction of the desired quality, which is the quality of fearlessness. It is not possible to transmute the vibration of fear into the vibration of a rose, or into the vibration of a potato, or into a crystal. You can *imbue* a rose or crystal with either fear or fearless because fear and fearless are qualities, not things. One quality can vibrate into and become the opposite quality. Once the quality changes, the physical form can change.

All true polarity is a matter of higher or lower vibration. Love and hate are a single line. Fear and fearless are a single line. There is no distinct separation in a polarity. There is no single place on the line where fear becomes fearless, where hate becomes love. Fear can change to fearless, and hate can change to love by changing the vibration of the line. How do you change the vibration of the line? *Focus your attention on the desired quality.* Point B is your desired quality. Point B is a higher vibration than Point A and as you focus more and more attention on Point B you create heat. Energy/heat raises the vibration of the line and changes Point A in the direction of the highest frequency of vibration which is Point B. The frequency of vibration at Point B becomes greater than Point A. Why? Because Point B is your clear intention and you focus your powerful attention there. This creates energy. Energy makes things happen.

Our Great Work is to change matter into Spirit. Matter and Spirit are opposite poles, separated only by degrees of vibration. If you focus energy at either point you raise its vibration and strengthen that point. Matter is Point A, your departure point, and Spirit is your point of arrival, Point B. Where do you want to focus your attention; your energy/heat? What is the desired quality? What do you want? The point you are paying the most attention to is the point that will come into being in your life.

Do you want fear? At Point A you have to ask yourself if you really do want the life you are experiencing. Do you want fear? Do you want unhappiness? Would you like to live from a constant, deeper, and wiser place, beyond your current existence? Look at those things in your life you worry about—things that scare you, things that make you angry, things that make you unhappy. This is your Point A. It is important to be clear when you create Point A because there is a part of you that doesn't want to change and resists changing. Part of you couldn't receive the change and wouldn't recognize it if it happened. Part of you would run away. Part of you would run back into your old existence because it is the known; it is safe. Part of you is programmed to resist new information. You have to be persistent with your quest. No matter what part of you is resisting the Mystery, repeat your choice over and over.

In their wonderful book on Sufi prayer entitled *The Illuminated Prayer,* Coleman Barks and Michael Green tell a story about a great Sufi teacher named Bawa Muhaiyaddeen. This teacher would ask everyone who came to him "What do you want?" Over and over, he would ask this question. The question would be a catalyst for the student's awakening. I call this question the God question. I first consciously heard this question—"What do you want?" during a Superconscious meditation. It came at me and my hair stood on end.

I learned through a series of meditations the importance of asking yourself the right question. I look at awakening as depending on finding the path of two questions: "Do you like the way you are/Do you like your life the way it is?" is the first question that must be looked at truly *and* "What do you want?" is the second question. And you might think about the question of being true to yourself. What is more important than Being True to Your Self? These questions have led me from awakening to awakening. Awakening is the unfolding of a thousand petals. Petal by petal your mind and heart open and merge with your Soul until you realize that mind, heart, soul, are only concepts. They are just words, and your direct experience of the Divine Source is beyond words.

At the beginning of my quest I would sometimes have, in a deep meditative state, an experience that I called *"the roar"*. In that "roar", I would experience a distinct sense of a voice outside of myself, coming from far away yet inside me and surrounding me. It was awesome, beautiful, unmistakable, and *believable.* The roar is beyond context or content. I had no teacher and no one I could ask about my experiences. I am grateful for this now but at the time it made me feel very isolated. I once asked a yoga teacher about this experience and he told me I was hallucinating. This made me realize that the experience was incommunicable and that I must live by faith—and to ask for help only from the Source of the roar—the absolute depth and stillness of the Christ Consciousness. This was my Reality.

I was asking for help and help came to me. I was brought into the presence of a teacher. He was teaching a class called DMA. I had never been to a workshop and I didn't go to psychics so I had never had a "reading" or attended a "spiritual" class. I took this class because on some deep level I recognized the teacher as having something I wanted. I took the class and I was stunned. I couldn't separate my own thoughts from the thought that had created the DMA system. I felt a sense of deliverance. Not because I was learning the DMA system but because I was learning how to form the teachings I already knew into a class. The teachings that I had received from Christ Consciousness had been haunting me, demanding expression. For years I had been trying to teach classes in manifesting and alchemy. I was clear about the teachings but each attempt to impart them was humiliating and disastrous. I didn't know how to teach. I was too afraid of people. I had agoraphobia. I had a serious illness, a lung disease. During my five or six weeks in the DMA class, all these illusions of fear and illness fell away from me. It was like coming face to face with my own mind. Or rather, it was like coming mind to mind with the Mind that had created both my mind and the DMA mind. Words and phrases that I had received through channeling and which I had thought were my own were in my ears constantly during that class. It was awesome. It validated everything I had been receiving from communion with my Beloved Sophia.

I tried to teach DMA but was unable to because I had too much of my own creativity involved in my own work, and I was continually being pulled into my own direction. But it was the beginning for me of acceptance of myself as a teacher. Every day when I thank God, and thank all teachers who have ever yearned for God, I also thank Robert Fritz, spiritual genius, the creator of the DMA system.

In those early days of discovery, I studied religious texts looking for answers to some of my Superconscious experiences. I would put my mind on something and receive whole increments of information while skimming a text. I was skimming through an article on the Vedas, I think it was by Rudolph Steiner, on the oversoul, kundalini and Shakti, and I caught a phrase that went something like "She" comes sometimes with a whisper, sometimes with a "*roar*". Again my hair stood on end.

I was filled with joy to learn that my experience of the roar of God—and the Beauty of Sophia—was not unique and isolated. Others had had the same experience of the whisper and the roar and named it—Shakti, Kundalini, the High Self, the Oversoul, the Superconscious. From then on I was able to continue into my own experience with more confidence and receive the full experience of the "roar", the voice of God and my Soul asking me, *Do you like the way you are?* Of course I didn't. I despised myself. It took some time before I could stand before that question and not cringe away from it. No, I did not like my life the way it was, and once I answered that question honestly I was able to deal with the next question, *What do you want?* roared at me by a loving Presence. I have always thought of those two questions as *the* Superconscious questions.

(I was such an innocent. I look back on myself and wonder how I survived my first experience of Superconscious Light. I was stumbling through some perilous waters. But as I look back on it, I realize that somehow I was prepared for the experience and those waters were not perilous for me because for me, there were no sharks. There was only relief. Such a magnitude of Light is only perilous to the untransformed ego and somehow, somewhere, my ego had already been through the Fire.

I had been all my life afraid of this human world of shadows—I was afraid to walk down the street, afraid to leave my house. I felt surrounded by fear and pain was an entity that walked with me.

And although I was able to become a fairly skilled actor on the stage of this world, I had never been able to let go of a kind of skin-crawling, disbelieving horror at what human beings are capable of in the way of creative cruelty. I did not feel prepared to be a citizen of the human world—"*No Demons Outside of Humanity*" is an anonymous Hermetic axiom and I felt that way. I readily believed in demonic humanity. So the roar held no fear for me, it was not perilous, it was home. It was safe. And it came to me; I didn't go looking for it but I was desperately praying for the roar of God—The One Source.)

I learned. Before you can ask yourself what you want, you have to deal with the question of do you like your life the way it is? Do you like the way you are? Are you willing to be true to yourself? This being true is a very old concept but few people have followed it as a spiritual path into a universe that is true beyond beliefs, beyond cultures, race, tribe or history. Shakespeare said it most beautifully, "This above all to thine own self be true," and it follows organically that if you are true to your Self, you cannot then be false to anyone. When you are honestly able to answer "Do you like the way your life is?" then you are ready for, "What do you want?" coming at you in a voice of thunder!

Imagine that we live in a universe that is constantly asking us the "What do you want?" question and giving us an equivalent answer. "What do I want?" is the most important question in the world. When you are creating your polarity, asking yourself these true questions over and over and searching for the honest answer brings you close to being true to yourself. Why? Because if you ask for truth, you have to let go of your inner ego commentary and just receive the truth about your life. Does anyone really want conflict and suffering? Yes. Some part of your ego-centered *identity* might *seem* to want to cling to suffering or conflict and this is why you must clear the boards by continually asking yourself the questions, "Do I like how I am?" and "What is it I *really* want?" and "Am I willing to be true to my Self no matter what that means or where it takes me?"

Be honest—for the polarity to be powerful, you must be honest with yourself. Don't waste energy having a dialogue with your past, with the old part of yourself. The past is the house that ego built. Do not think you have to tear that house down. Do not fight with your ego. Let it be. Just don't feed it. Don't let the part of you that is attached to old beliefs, old stories, old fears, and old trauma sabotage your work of art. Don't stand around talking about and being anxious about the journey, just get on the train.

Keep your mind on the stars but keep your eyes on your footsteps. (*The Kybalion*) This means be aware of your departure point at the same time you are aware of your highest intentions and at the same time aware of the path under your feet. Learn to be multidimensional in your attention. Be in many places at once. Don't try to control the path, just take the first step. Let go of thinking about your process but be aware of the journeying. Be aware of what choices you are making as you go. The Hermetic teachings warn against misunderstanding the principle of polarity—beware of omitting either side of the paradox—beware of half-truths. Be honest about your departure (Do you like the way you are?) and be honest about where you want to arrive. (What do you want?). Being honest about your arrival means you don't limit your ideals. But at the same time don't project outcomes and don't predict how the outcome you want has to arrive; don't try to control the journey.

Don't try to keep your imagination within the limits of your beliefs. It doesn't matter if you believe you lack something, what matters is that you acknowledge that feeling that something vital is missing in your life. What matters is at some level you know that this feeling is not truth. There is something you want, but you can't pin it down—what it is or how to make it happen. You don't have to know what it is. It is the call of your Spirit. Choose to receive your real life, your true existence, and your Spirit will bring it to you. It doesn't matter if you believe that you are not beautiful; choose to receive your own beauty. It doesn't matter if you believe you are less intelligent than your friends; choose to receive your own intelligence. It doesn't matter if you believe you are not good at taking care of yourself; choose to be good at taking care of yourself. Open the door to your truth. But don't describe how beauty should look, or how truth should be, or how taking care of yourself should happen. And do not compare yourself to others. Don't try to describe what intelligence or beauty is; just say you want it and that you are willing to receive it, and don't keep looking behind you at your old library of don't, can't, and mustn't. Keep your eye on the quality you want. Dr. King gave us a famous and effective clue when he declared, "Keep your eye on the prize." Dr. King also said it is not necessary to see the whole stairway, just take the first step and don't try to control the process or be attached to outcomes, to what might be at the top of the stairs. Do not project. Just proceed.

Learn to think in a new way. Look at these places where your old attention has been focused—the places where things are wrong in your life—the *I won't have anything good and I won't be all right unless I fix it, and there is no way to fix my life, I'm too old, it's too late, I'm too sick, I'm too tired, it's hopeless.* You know, *those* places—the places where you have been lax and lazy and fearful, have been obsessing on what you lack. The places where you have been attached to victim, to wounded love, to evaluating damage and obsessing on damage.

Do you like this the way it is? Do you want these things changed? When you think about change, and you think in the old way, a linear, controlling, mental way, do you feel dread, drained, anxious, and hopelessly burdened? Do you feel that change requires a lot of work and time, and that you just don't have the energy and time? It doesn't matter if you feel this way; take the first step, then take another step, get on the train. One step at a time; one stair at a time; one petal at a time; the change creates itself. Your new existence unfolds in divine order and the timing is perfect.

So your first practice in Real Magic, as you create your polarity, is to practice letting go of your old way of thinking about change. The old linear, mental *control* way of thinking is to focus on process. Do not *think about process.* Let go of process. The clue to thinking in a new, creative way is *do not process* the ways in which change can or can't happen or the ways that your stress can be resolved. Let go of anxiety about outcomes, about *how* to fix your hopeless problem. Let go of the outcome. Creation is not goal oriented, it is creation oriented. Creation is an ongoing light show. *Practice the secret of letting go.* The secret of letting go is to let go of *outcomes.* Let go of anxiety about outcomes. Let go of trying to process and manipulate outcomes. Let go of *ownership*, as if you own the outcome and have to cling to it and control it. Let go of taking outcomes *personally.* Let go of outcomes.

Let go of process. Do not process and try to control *how* the train is going to arrive at Point B. Do not process or obsess on old train-wreck stories. Stop processing your old stories about your wounds, your failures, and your victimization. Do not process possible dire outcome stories learned from the past or from the media, or from your neighbors and friends. You already know everything you need to know about your old existence. You and no one else knows the trouble you've seen. You know everything you need to know about your victim self. You don't have to keep processing the same old stories hoping for some miraculous change. Just look at the story you have been telling yourself. Often your old story will be a story about damage with you as a victim. Don't let yourself repeat that story anymore—just say to yourself, *This is my old story. This is not the story I want.* Say to yourself, *I don't like my life the way it is. I don't want to be unhappy, sick, scared and feel like a failure, I don't want to feel like a victim. I don't want to live in an atmosphere of lack and distrust. I do not want a marginal existence.* And by marginal existence, I mean a state of being. You could be a billionaire many times over and still be in a state of marginal existence. Once you make this declaration to yourself that you are willing to let go of your old story, say nothing more to yourself about it. All you need to know about Point A is that your old story is a lump of coal and you don't want that lump of coal. All you need to know is that your stress about any part of your life, is the fuel you would like to transmute in the Fire.

Write "Point A—departure" on one side of a sheet of paper and "Point B—arrival" on the other side of the sheet of paper. Define the lump of coal, the thing you want changed in your old existence and write it down at Point A. Then move on to Point B and at Point B, define the change you want, the diamond, the new existence and write it down.

Point B is the point of manifestation. New reality. Point B is the other part of the polarity, the opposite of Point A. Point B gives you a strong intention. A strong intention is crucial in manifesting. A lack of strong intention is like having no skeleton or trying to build a house with no blueprint and no foundation or frame. Departure—Arrival. You have the polarity. Old story—new intention. You now have a structure of departure and arrival. What do you do next?

You apply heat to Point B. How do you apply heat? *You focus your attention on the new intention that you have stated in writing at Point B.* It is your focused attention that provides the energy that puts flesh on the bones, shapes a house around the framework. Without the focus of your attention, your intention just falls away into vague yearnings and "maybe someday I'll win the lottery, maybe someday . . ." and you stay stuck in your old existence. Focused attention creates tremendous amounts of energy. Energy is heat. You apply that heat to Point B.

Now, you have intention at Point B and you want to keep your attention focused there all the time. How do you best do that? Do you think about it a lot? *No!* Don't think about it at all. You take that intention and turn it into a Word of Power. How? You turn it into a mantra and use that mantra as a daily spiritual practice. Create a mantra about each thing in your existence you would like to change, about anything you feel you lack. Then commune with your mantras every time you are tempted to think in the old way about your "trash". Remember your polarity of A-*depart* and B-*arrive.* Call your treasure to you by calling your mantra. This approach to stress, this new way of thinking, gives your old, doubting, anxious, controlling mind something new, creative, and productive to do.

To create a mantra you use the word "choose". The phrase "I choose" is a powerful agreement. This tells you that you are making a strong agreement with God, that you are willing to receive the new reality. "I *choose* to receive . . ." It is like saying to God, "I am willing to cooperate. I am willing to stand here before Creation and receive blessing". This is your answer to the thundering question, the "WHAT DO YOU WANT?" question "I am willing. Give me What I Am" is your answer to the roar.

Then what do you do?

You practice—and practice and practice. Repeated practice creates *creative tension.* I first heard the phrase *creative tension* from Dr. Martin Luther King Jr. He described creative tension as harmonious and stress free, as the energy that must be created before a new form can come into being. *(And this phrase, creative tension, came to epitomize for me the creative field of being that existed in the 1960s. It sometimes seemed, during that time, that all you had to do was think something and turn around, and there it would be, in front of you. It was an incredibly vital, creative, tense and intense time in history. A great time of the Great Work. An awful time. A blessed time.)*

As you practice spiritual practices, you create a tension that is the opposite of stress. This creative tension is an elastic, balanced tension, and it attracts energy and easily brings into being the form you want to manifest. Every artist is familiar with creative tension. If you don't practice and maintain creative tension, your new reality remains only a theory, and a theory is only a story *about* something. You have to practice. Practice creates the energy necessary for an artist to incorporate their craft. *Real* magic is an improvisation that arises organically once the sacred technology, the craft involved in creating, is incorporated as natural. Incorporating a craft comes by practicing the principles and techniques over and over. Whether it is a musical scale, mixing paints, or learning meditation, it must be practiced until it becomes second nature. Practice changes stress tension to creative tension. Creative tension builds energy. Energy makes things happen. Creative tension keeps the gift moving and moves the gift into place.

Repeat. How do you apply heat? You focus the power of your attention. What do you focus it on? A strong intention. How do you best do that? You create a Word of Power—a mantra. Many mantras. Call your mantras ceremoniously, in an attentive way, over and over, every day. Practice remembering that you are changing your existence. Practice remembering your intentions all the time. Keep your eye on the stars. Keep your feet on the ground. Keep a Point B list and recite it every day. Make your Point A list into mantras of letting go, and every day choose to let go of your "departure" list.

Learn to make lists. I have never made lists. When I first began my teaching attempts I pondered the principle of polarity for months. I had learned it as an esoteric concept and it rang true, but I could not grasp a way to teach people how to apply it in their daily life because the concept of making lists was foreign to me. Make lists, make *no/yes* lists, make *don't want/do want* lists. It was such a simple idea that I was stunned by it. Once I learned how to apply list making to the principle of polarity I could create the other Course practices.

The most powerful practice in the Course is something I call power points. In the old esoteric teachings, moments of overwhelming despair, self-pity, fear, or anger were called "vital moments". A student in a Mystery School was expected to master the energy of those vital moments. I call these vital moments power points. A power point is a point in your life when you feel really bad, grieving, enraged, desperate, or hopeless. You are overwhelmed by the emotion of the moment. To practice power pointing, first of all do not focus on controlling or repressing the intense emotions you are feeling. On the other hand, do not indulge in the emotions. When you find yourself in a vital moment, stop everything. Do something new with your consciousness. Think in a new way.

When you feel most stressed, you are powerful. A power point is filled with intense powerful energy. You can take that energy and shift it, turn it toward a new intention and make it work for you. You can transmute a lot of old energy if you learn to utilize power points. You are a polarity. In a power point, when you recognize that you are in a vital moment, shift your attention to Point B and apply heat. Put everything you've got into calling a mantra. Any mantra will do. Just think "Point B" if you are feeling seriously overwhelmed by old anger, pain or addiction. Or think "vital moment" to yourself. If you can remember this while you are in the throes, in the moment, you will master the secret of power. Power comes from recognizing your moments of stress as moments of vital energy that can work in your behalf. Your old existence is the fuel. A power point is a moment of powerful transmutation.

Practicing power points teaches you to live in the moment without ever once having to think about what living in the moment means or how to do it. Don't try. Forget about processing the moment; as soon as you think about the moment, it is gone. Practice noticing your power points and utilizing your creative power in those moments when you feel most powerless. As you master power points you will find yourself present and aware in each moment of your existence.

The polarity that exists within you is the disparity between your ego and your Spirit, between wounded love and unconditional love. A sense of separation and lack underlies all manifestation coming through an ego-oriented state of being. The ego-centered act of manifesting often begins with a focus on pain, on what you lack, on how you can get your needs met and fix all your problems. This focus perpetuates neediness or what we call "victim". Neediness leads to attachment, even obsession with what you think you need. Neediness, or victim mentality, perpetuates the desolation that comes from believing that lack is *real.* The despair or rage that comes when your expectations are disappointed feeds your belief in lack. Let go. Believe this: everything you need already exists and your essence, your Essential Self is not separate from it.

Being true to your Essential Self is ultimately the only Law of Manifestation. This is a cosmic law and is *infallible* in its workings. As you practice Truth, you experience an ongoing spiritual path created by shifts in your own awareness. Change doesn't come from outside of you. You are able to be whatever your awareness allows. If your awareness encompasses your Self, then you will be integrated—whole. By developing self-awareness through the experiences that emerge from your *conscious* choices, you learn to access your wholeness and as you let go of separation, you merge with the Divine Source, the Living Light that permeates existence. You become the *choiceless choice*. The pathless path. You *become* Freedom.

The process toward self-knowledge can be long and painful or a wonderful creative adventure depending on the importance you give to your ego and on the choices you make in each moment. You exist in an ocean of endless possibility. From this ocean of choices, perceptions, reactions, feelings, thoughts, practices, and new experience, there develops an incorporation and distillation of new experience—a state of self-knowledge that embodies your truth. Do you want to manifest your true intentions, to know why you came here? Do you even know what kind of life you truly desire to live? Do you want your real life? Begin anywhere and do not try to judge your beginning—just depart at Point A. A conscious beginning will lead you to your arrival, to merging, to radiant awareness and Freedom. Radiance is your true nature. Radiant awareness is your true state of being. Freedom is your birthright. You are God's beautiful Dream and God's beautiful Dreamer. Be true to that by choosing to be true to yourself. It really is that simple. It's real magic.

CHAPTER 4

THE MOST POWERFUL THING YOU HAVE

WHAT IS THE most powerful thing you have?

People in classes answer this question in many different ways and usually in terms of skill and talent. "The most powerful thing I have is my talent for music." "The most powerful thing I have is my computer skill." "The most powerful thing I have is my athletic ability . . . my power to make conscious choices . . . my power is my love for my children . . . my intelligence . . . my education . . . my spirituality . . . love . . ."

Wrong. The most powerful thing you have is your *attention.* Combine this, the most powerful thing you have, with the most powerful force in the Universe, which is the force of *intention* and you have power. Power comes from your ability to *focus* attention and maintain that focus toward an intention. Focus is a powerful tool. When you say "focus" you are talking about attention. If you say someone is focused, you are saying that his or her attention is focused.

ATTENTION

One may change his mental vibration by an effort of Will in the direction of deliberately fixing Attention upon a more desirable state.
Will directs the Attention, and Attention changes the Vibration.
Cultivate the Art of Attention, by means of the Will, and you have solved the secret of the Mastery of Moods.

The Kybalion

The study of metaphysics teaches that thought creates form and the thoughts you carry right now are creating your future. I think, to be accurate, we must say it is the intention held within and sent forth from our thoughts that creates our future. This intention is coming from the places in our consciousness where our attention is most strongly focused. This is why obsession is so powerful. Obsessive thoughts are beaming out a focused *intention* that is gathering energy around itself. Our thoughts are a mirror of our attention, both our conscious and in most cases, our subconscious attention. Thought *is* our attention. Thought tells you where your attention is most strongly directed. In the Real Magic Course, we use the concept of attention as a tool, a way in which to work consciously with our thoughts.

The most powerful thing you have is your attention. People who are successful are successful because their attention is focused like a single beam on the thing they want. Like a great actor focused on the effect they want to create, successful people, focusing their attention, become the thing they want and bring it into being. This is a subtle process. What is attention? Is it definable? Is attention the same thing as attentive?

Most people think attention is about thinking. Attention is not thinking. An attentive mind is not a thinking mind. A thinking mind is a busy mind. A thinking mind is an *interpretive* mind. A thinking mind is an analytical mind. An *attentive* mind is very quiet—not interpreting or analyzing; it simply notices the present—observes what *is* without commenting on what was or what should be. An attentive mind is both at rest and active at the same time. A focused attention is immediate, in the present moment—now. It is not looking at yesterday or tomorrow. A focused attention is an attention that includes all the senses, both physical and subtle. When your attention is focused, it is as if you are reaching out an invisible beam of light and touching that which you are focused on. You are not *thinking about how to interpret* the thing you are focused on; you are just touching it. And you are touching it with the totality of yourself. So a focused attention is not a commentary and it does not include interpretation; it is an *action.* It is akin to the action of listening carefully, with all your senses, your whole self, still and poised and ready to receive.

Your focused attention is like a magnet. It creates a concentrated energy field around a focal point and the focal point attracts and "gathers" more and more energy. This is why obsession is so dangerous. Obsession creates tremendous amounts of energy around a focal point. And this is why the human tendency to cling to whatever feeling we are locked into or believe is true can be dangerous. Tremendous energy gathers around the place where your attention is focused. And energy *makes things happen!*

Learning to focus your attention allows you to work *with* rather than against your imagination and emotions. Staying focused on a new intention gives your attention work to do that allows you to stay unattached to what happened in the past and not afraid of or projecting what will happen tomorrow. Obsessing on the past simply energizes past damage and prevents a new future from manifesting. If your gaze is always toward the past, it prevents you from seeing the truth of right now; the moment's truth passes you by because you are in yesterday's story and yesterday's story makes you anxious about tomorrow's story. When your attention is focused on yesterday's news, you will continue to manifest yesterday's stories in new forms—tomorrows outcomes will mirror past outcomes. Your patterns of energy do not change unless you take the time to shift your attention to a new template.

ESSAY ON ATTENTION FROM THE REAL MAGIC COURSE:

What is attention? The Latin root of the word attention means "to reach out; to stretch out". The act of attention is the act of reaching out; an *extension* and *expansion* of the senses that allows human beings to physically, emotionally, mentally, and psychically, know their environment. Attention has to do with mind. There are two kinds of mind: attentive mind and controlling mind. Controlling mind is the part of mind that we would call "normal". A controlling mind is interpretive. It is not observing fully; it is busy *interpreting* the environment with the intention of *controlling* the environment. This is not necessarily bad but it is a limited use of mind power. Attentive mind has to do with *knowing* the environment. And such knowing comes in complete increments of knowledge that do not need mental interpretation.

An attentive mind is a *free* mind. It is not focused on control so it is free to receive. Therefore, attentive mind is a receptive mind. Attention is not thinking. Attention is not intellectual. Attention is not judgmental. Attention is a form of listening, of reciprocity—giving and receiving. Attention is not a mental intensification; it is a mental relaxation and expansion. When you are attentive you are receiving and observing without interpreting. You are free.

If you are interpreting, you are thinking *about*. Thinking about is a mental process of looking for meaning, comparing, evaluating, and analyzing. This process is usually focused on some particular outcome or goal. If you are thinking about outcomes, you are not free to be attentive. Attention is not about outcomes. Attention is always in the moment.

Attention is powerful because attention is the faculty in yourself which allows you to focus energy. If you have trained yourself to focus, you can focus in any direction and *receive back* information, revelation or knowledge. Attention is non-personal. Think of your attention as an eye, or a beam of energy that you can direct anywhere. Imagine focusing this beam through your mind and senses and wherever you direct it, your focus will create energy, and information will come back to you along that beam of attention. It is a powerful and impersonal tool that requires your whole self and uses all your senses without bias or interpretation.

To utilize your attention you must let go of judgment, let go of comparing, interpreting, and analyzing and just be present. When you pay attention in this way, you receive data that is correct because it is not attached to your emotional expectations. Paying attention expands your awareness of yourself and leads to revelation, discernment, and wisdom. Revelation is *silent* knowledge. Silence requires your attention and not your intellect. Discernment means wise and accurate observation of what *is* without any attachment to what was or what should or could be, without any "if only" or any attachment to a particular outcome. Wisdom is not definable; wisdom is wisdom. Thinking about and figuring out do not expand your awareness, it leads to more thinking about. This is why I ask you not to take notes in class. Practice listening with your attention and not with your controlling, interpretive mind.

Attention is observation. Attention is both relaxed and active. Attention is listen, look, receive what is, receive impressions without interpreting or looking for an answer, or trying to make a judgment. This is observation. Observation means to notice fully without *thinking about* what you are noticing. Notice *what is* without thinking about what is. At the same time, observation includes an understanding of the situation one is observing—or a willingness to suspend judgment while waiting on the understanding. This allows Truth to come to you. This creates discernment. If you are silently noticing what is, truth shows up.

FOCUSING

Attention includes the ability to focus. In the Course, I give two handouts attention and focusing as a matching set.

Focusing is not a mental activity. In all esoteric schools, focusing means using your consciousness in specific ways that can strengthen your capacity to raise and contain—create and hold—energy. Mystery School students are successful because their attention is continually focused on their intention, while continually releasing any energy toward manipulating or trying to control outcomes. In this way, they can raise and hold tremendous amounts of energy and keep it moving toward a creative completion. Staying present in your intention while releasing outcomes enables you to utilize all the available energy of each moment.

Focusing your attention means focusing your *awareness.* It is as if you have antennae all over your body, and you are expanding all of your antennae. This kind of focusing does *not* mean a *narrowing* of your attention or a mental concentration. It is an *expansion,* a relaxing of mental *interpretation,* which allows new thoughts, emotions, intuitions, and sensations *to be received.* Focused attention creates a quiet mind—an *empty mind,* a quietness that unfolds and expands awareness. Focus is receptive; it is about receiving.

Focusing does not require mental intensity or mental concentration. It does not require effort or strain. It does not take from your energy; it gives you energy. Focused attention is *silent.* The ability to focus your attention gives you the freedom to experience what Krishnamurti called a "vast space" in the brain in which there is unimaginable energy, tremendous energy—and which I call the Superconscious or the Christ Consciousness—the Silence of the Christ.

SOME SUGGESTIONS FOR PRACTICING FOCUS:

All human beings are creative. All human beings are able to transmute energy. Learning to focus your attention leads to expanded awareness, expanded creativity, and awakens your ability to transmute energy. Learning to focus requires daily practice. It is rather like going into a gym every day and working out.

Focusing is a different form of seeing than we are taught. Most of us "see" with our emotions. Practice seeing with your attention rather than with your emotions. For example, when you first walk into a room you've never been in, you receive an impression and that impression is primarily emotional and comes from what you believe is true about yourself in the world, or about yourself walking into this room. This is very subjective.

Walk into the room and practice observing the room with no emotional judgments. Look with your attentive eye. For example, with your attentive eye, you might see that the window drapes are gray, the walls are light green, there is a display of live plants and pottery along the west wall, and the windows face north. You would look with no intention except to know your environment. With your emotional eye you would be creating a constant judgmental commentary, such as "Oof, gray, I hate the color gray . . . Wonder why they put gray drapes with a green wall . . . How ugly is that . . ." You might be trying to be attentive but your emotions are ad-libbing, "I don't like green for walls . . . at least not that shade . . . too much yellow . . . Those drapes don't do well with yellow . . . What's with these people . . . No color sense . . ." This is your emotional eye and your ego making a judgment whether to accept the people who live in this room—you are deciding whether to see them as uncomfortable and possibly dangerous others or to accept them as possible friends.

Practice looking at places and things with a deliberate attention eye, then shift and deliberately *include* your emotional commentary and see what knowledge about *yourself* is revealed. Another practice is when you find yourself seeing with your emotional eye, shift to your attentive eye and notice what changes. This is a good practice in noticing how judgmental you actually are. It gives you the opportunity to let go of your judgmental eye and practice discernment instead. Do this playfully and practice not taking this exercise *personally.* This is practice.

Practice stopping all activity several times a day and silently be aware of your inner and outer environment. Don't try to do this in any particular way, or do it the "right" way. Just stop and look and listen with your attention without trying to interpret what anything means. Can you see how this kind of focus requires all your senses? Sit very quietly. Close your eyes and imagine yourself reaching out with your attention and touching parts of the environment. For example, close your eyes and reach out and touch various objects in the room. Then, keeping your eyes closed, reach with your attention to another room and touch the objects in that room. If you need to remember the room open your eyes and notice the room then close your eyes and reach out with your attention. Touch the ceiling above your head and then touch the floor under your feet

Then continue this practice with different parts of your body. With your attention, touch your big toe, then both big toes at once, then both feet. Practice holding and balancing your attention, keeping it firmly in one place until you feel balanced. Imagine that training your attention is like training a puppy, it keeps wandering off, and you calmly and patiently bring it back. Your attention will jump around, just keep bringing it back until it "takes." Once you have got your attention balanced at one place, practice shifting to another place, a different part of your body. Touch the back of your head with your attention and see how long you can hold your attention in place. Then shift to the top of your head and hold your attention there until it "takes." Then go somewhere else, for example, to your left elbow, then to your right hand. With each shift in your focus, see how long you can hold your attention in place.

Practice shifting from one side of your body to the other. Start at the top of your head and move back and forth from one side of your body to the other side starting at the top of your head and working down to your toes. For example, move from head to shoulders—left shoulder, right shoulder, to hands, left-right, to hips, to knees, to feet. Then focus all your attention on both feet at once, then both knees at once, then both hips, shoulders, and hands, then to your head. Now, rest in your body, relaxed and allowing a feeling of well-being to pour through you.

Play with this. Be playful with these exercises; they are surprisingly potent.

Then practice focusing on various distances, placing your focused attention about one inch above, in front of, or behind, various parts of your body and holding it there. Don't focus on getting an exact measurement, approximate the distance. For example, shift from one inch above your head (or one inch above the palm of your hand), to two feet, then about three feet, then more feet, six feet . . ., each time feeling out an approximate distance, getting a feel for it and balancing and holding your attention there.

Then go inward, focus your attention on your liver, on your stomach, on your heart. Each time practice approximating, balancing, and holding the energy in one place for a good moment. Then shift and practice focusing on your own energy field. For example, focus attention one-by-one on each of your chakras as if you are bringing your chakras into balance. If you do not work with your chakras, take your attention and focus first on the top of your head, then on your forehead, then on the back of your head, then on the tip of your nose, then on your throat, then at the center of your chest, then between your shoulder blades, then on your solar plexus, then on your lower stomach just below your navel—or focus on your navel, and then at the base of your spine. At each place, once you bring your attention into balance, see how long you can hold your attention there and keep it balanced. Practice harmony as if your total body, both your subtle energy body and physical body, is a musical instrument, and you are tuning it, getting ready for a performance. As you focus on various parts, try humming a tone, any tone; let the tone come to you.

This is a very good exercise to do. It balances the left and right sides of your energy field and then aligns your center. Do this with the same attention you would give to a physical workout. If you do physical exercise or workout, take a moment to do an attention work out. When you have become adept at holding focused attention on one point, go on to an advanced Attention workout, and try holding your focused attention on two places at once. Then on more than two places at once. Try focusing on your left big toe and right elbow while carrying on a conversation with a friend. Or try focusing an inch above your head and an inch outside the center of your chest while listening to music, or focus on both hands, or on any two parts of the body, while listening to sounds in your environment. Practice reaching out with your attention and touching two or more trees at once. Practice touching and sensing the natural world, trees, rocks, water, flowers. Practice attentive silence, inner and outer silence. Use your total environment as a place to practice attention.

Try focusing an inch above your head and at the back of your head simultaneously. Try focusing on your left and right hands while focusing at the top of your head. Left and right hands and the top of your head make a trinity, three points of focus. If you can hold this focus long enough, you might see a triangle forming itself in the energy between these three points. Students doing this practice have seen different forms of triangle, from delicate filaments of light appearing between their hands and meeting at the top of their head, to solid sheets of gold appearing and disappearing and moving all the way to the horizon.

This triangle is the beginning of deep meditation and, if you like, can be used in your meditation practices. You can use these focusing practices to center yourself, then continue the practice and, creating a triangle, focus on the triangle, allowing it to change as it will, until it disappears and a feeling of wholeness and peace encompasses you. You might do this as a practice that accompanies your mantras. Do some attention focusing practices until you feel centered and then repeat your mantras to yourself. This is a good way to experience the shifts in energy that occur as you recite your mantras.

Utilizing a daily attention focusing practice helps you to feel more in touch with yourself. It expands your awareness until you become more in touch with what it is you actually do want in your real life. A daily attention meditation expands your awareness of your wholeness and leads to revelations about yourself that encourage you to trust the practice of being true to yourself. You become aware that there is nothing more important than self-knowledge. You find that many fears and beliefs, desire and neediness, just fall away from you as you practice making deliberate choices and utilizing deliberate attention. You learn that the only thing you ever really wanted was to love and be wise and *that* is the truth about abundance—love and wisdom. You will find that once you are truly in touch with your Self, you will need no more concepts or practices or courses and classes. Inner peace and a feeling of completeness, of integrity, are, after all, the goal of transformation. Real magic leads you to simplicity and wisdom. It leads you to freedom. And most of all, it leads you to the understanding that when you are in a state of freedom, there is nothing you lack.

CHAPTER 5

THE POWER OF THE WORD: THE LAW OF DEFINITION

REPETITION IS POWERFUL. Your *repeated* thoughts and feelings form blueprints for bringing into your life equivalent experiences. Your persistent thoughts and feelings are equivalent to a powerful *intention.* You are holding powerful intentions in your subconscious that come from old *definitions*—old conclusions you have made about yourself and the world. You can reverse these old intentions by consciously utilizing a universal law called the Law of Definition.

If you study traditional alchemy or shamanism or any kind of ritual magic you are going to run into a lot of rules about the right way to do things. These rules are called the Laws of Magic. All the laws that surround the various forms of magic came into being because the ancient alchemists and teachers understood something called the Law of Definition. From the Law of Definition they created a lot of laws that they defined as the Laws of Magic. As a species we have evolved. As we've evolved, we've moved through spiritual stages and change until we have reached a point in human consciousness where the old shamanistic beliefs and practices are outdated and, because they have become fixed and rigid belief systems, even undermine our present attempts to live consciously. They act as a distraction away from the simplicity of truth. Although many of these laws are now archaic, the Law of Definition is always true and applicable because it is a universal principle.

What is a definition? The dictionary says that a definition is a statement of what a thing *is.* The Law of Definition states that *any* definition—that means description, thought, image, idea, feeling about, or statement of what a thing is—that you *receive* and *hold*—that you repeat over and over in your consciousness, will manifest in your life in some equivalent form. That means any description, anything that has impacted you so much that you dwell on it, anything you obsess on, any experience that you repeatedly describe, any continually repeated thought, whether it be about beauty and goodness, or greed and fear—angels or demons—if you are attached to it, if you cling to it, if you dwell on it and repeat it over and over, it will create a real equivalent form in your physical world. You are calling it into being and it will become "real" in your life. This is where the concept of Words of Power comes from.

A *focused* intention is equivalent to a Word of Power. This is the law. When you repeatedly focus attention on and "call" a Word, Creation responds with an equivalent Word. Words have Power—we live in a universe that responds to our most powerful definitions. Call and response. The New Testament book of John declares, "In the beginning was the Word." Jesus was the Incarnate Word. Ask and ye shall receive is the truth about Creation.

ESSAY ON THE LAW OF DEFINITION FROM THE REAL MAGIC COURSE:

The Law of Definition is a cosmic law and you can find it stated in some form in most religious texts and all studies of alchemy and magic. This cosmic law is referred to obliquely in each of the *innumerable* laws of magic. This cosmic law is the foundation of everything I teach.

The Law of Definition is precise. It means what it says. It declares that beliefs, fears, hopes, dreams, thoughts, emotions and such, are *conclusions*—definitions of reality that you carry in your conscious and unconscious self. The definitions that receive the most repetitive, the most constant, the most focused attention from you are the definitions that will manifest as a reality in your life. In other words, once you define something it has existence and will manifest physically if it is given a strong repetitive mental and emotional attention. And that attention can be a conscious mantra or an unconscious belief. Either way the Law holds true.

This Law is where the concept of Words of Power comes from. This is where the belief in chanting as a powerful tool comes from. This is where "Be Careful What You Ask For" comes from. This is where the French/African word *conjure* comes from—this word literally means, "call into being." The Law of Definition is responsible for the magical axiom and warning, *"A Thing Becomes What It Is Repeatedly Called."*. The Law of Definition represents responsibility in the truest sense of the word—call and response—your ability to respond instantly and creatively to anything you meet on your life path.

Pay attention to how you are defining the world, for your definitions will manifest in the environment around you. Observe how you define your self in your world and you will understand the patterns that make up your life. Listen to yourself as you speak and you will begin to cultivate a strong desire to make sure your words and thoughts match the vision in your heart of the kind of world you would like to live in.

There is a story about the Soul in the old esoteric traditions. Students are taught that when the Soul desires to create a change, she (the Soul is "She" in many ancient traditions) "throws" a Word—a thought-form image of the change—out in front of her, and it attracts energy to itself and becomes a reality in the life of the person. You walk straight into the catalyst for change that your Soul has defined and called into being. This is manifesting.

In the Course I use the concept of a mantra to convey the power of the Word. Mantra is a Sanskrit word, which means literally "thought-sound". A mantra is a spiritual tool, a way to hold a defined thought-form in place and use it as an agent for transformation. A mantra holds a Word of Power, When you use a mantra you are consciously throwing forth a Word that holds an image of the quality or thing that you want—and that Word will come alive and in some equivalent form, show up in your life.

In West Africa I literally observed the power of the Word used as a tool to call up an ancient thought form. I was traveling with a group of healers and psychologists from the United States. We were invited as guests of a master shaman to attend a panther ceremony. This was an initiation ceremony for adolescent boys. The purpose of the initiation was to fill the boys with the spirit of the panther. The ceremony utilized rhythm, chanting, and dancing. Musicians sat in a semicircle playing an instrument that was similar to an upright bass as it is played in jazz. They were using it both as a drum and as a stringed instrument of eloquent harmony. The sounds they made were very repetitious and quite beautiful. As the musicians worked, the shaman would at intervals repeat a call that sounded remarkably like a panther. It was a chilling sound, and the combination of rhythm and this panther call was riveting. At intervals and responding to an internal call and response, the boys one at a time would feel moved to get up and dance their personal panther dance.

After each boy had danced, the boys stood and moving as one, began a dance that had a subtly different rhythm. The music didn't change, but one of the drummers began to strike an instrument that looked like an iron stick with iron cowbells and pieces of iron loosely attached to it. It was both clashing and rhythmic, and it added a different rhythm to the mix, a rhythm that I felt as rippling or stealthy. I felt this rhythm as an indescribable physical feeling. It seemed to ripple through my spine and bloodstream. It seemed that the boys were moving to all the different sounds at once but in a very rhythmic fluid way. Suddenly I became aware of a *presence.* It was hovering as if in the air above us, without shape or any kind of form really, yet I was aware of a sense of shape and a feeling that this shape was questing. That is how I defined it to myself when I became aware of it. It was like a cat moving its head around questing, testing the air. I have a distinct memory of it, but like most astral form, I was actually seeing it in my mind's eye and my body was sensing it. When one is present, face-to-face with such a distinctive astral form, it awakens a sense of both wonder and instant acceptance and time feels suspended. Time is nonexistent.

Such experiences are not frightening. I felt no fear. It was all very silent. I simply felt a knowingness about what was happening. But it was all very fast and very quiet and I would have been hard put to articulate the sensation. I sensed the presence look at me. That was what it felt like, as if it had sensed me and looked at me and paused. This was very difficult to put into words; there was a moment of stillness or pause, something indescribable, then it was as if I reached out with my mind—my attention—and turned it away from me. There was a moment, very still, very powerful, suspended, of acknowledgment, and it moved on. I immediately looked away, retreated into myself. It seemed intrusive to project anything into that moment. The "panther" belonged to that culture and to those boys.

When I turned my attention away from that sense of presence, it stopped existing. This was literal, as if the world shifted and I could see and sense no more of the ceremony. I was back in the uncomfortably hot sun and repetitious noise. I knew that no one in the group I was with had noticed anything. It was a very private experience until I became aware of the master shaman, the man who had brought us as guests to this ceremony. I felt him and turned around and he was looking at me and laughing very hard. When later I asked him what had been so funny he said that when the panther spirit sensed my presence and paused, it looked to him as if I reached out and patted it on its head and sent it on its way. He explained to me that it was my awareness of the presence that had directed its attention to me but I was not trained in the habitual and programmed responses therefore, an "emptiness", a non-response happened and it moved on.

It was a beautiful experience. I felt both honored and awed by it. To the Africans it was a panther spirit. To me it was the miracle of observing the Law of Definition in action. Eons ago, powerful shamans, attuned to the reality—blood, bones, sinew, and life force—of the panther, had created a ceremony to strengthen the young men of their people. They created a thought form that held all the attributes of panther and with the permission and cooperation of the panther spirit, and through repeated use, the thought form became an astral entity, a programmed intention of divine proportion. It was beautiful.

This was power. The Law of Definition and Word of Power. This thought-form was ancient. They, the shamans, musicians, and drummers had been calling it for unknown centuries. It was the astral form of a powerful and powerfully defined intention. It had been created to serve a powerful purpose and that purpose was to imbue those boys with a sense of maturity, courage, and totem intelligence. Totems in these forms of astral programming—astral definition—have been worshipped for countless centuries on this planet and they are real. They once served a vital purpose as teachers and healers within a tribal ecology. It was for me a validation of a teaching I had been trying very hard to understand beyond my intellectual appreciation of it. The Law of Definition. And I understood that in the particular way I was using mantras in my teaching I was doing what teachers have done since the first spiritual teacher walked the planet—utilizing the power of the Word. I know that for my students, things happen when they begin to repeat a mantra like, "I Choose To Receive Peace."

One of the things that can happen when you begin to use mantras that state powerful new intentions is *resistance* from your ego. Imagine that you have created some life mantras and you are repeating them ceremoniously every day. What happens when you first begin to repeat your mantras, your Words of strong intention? Often your *egoic* consciousness senses the *accelerated energy* of the new intention and begins to *protect* you from the *acceleration*. You feel resistance. This is not a bad thing, to check out new information; to be critical is a good quality but this must be accompanied by a willingness to be open, to experiment and receive new experience. If you consciously practice humility by saying to yourself that you don't know how, but you want to be real, you want your true life so you will be open in spite of this fear you are feeling, or in spite of this arrogance you are feeling, you will relax into the new feeling or the new experience and you will remember that there are new ways you can use thought and ways you can effectively practice your truth.

There are practices you can consciously use when you feel resistance, resentment or fear. You are trying to create faith and success within a world programmed and shaped by past beliefs and fear, and driven by this consciousness called ego. There is a lot of old fixed energy that you have to deal with. What do you do? Do you try to reason with yourself? Do you try to analyze your resistance? Do you condemn yourself and try to fix things? No.

You use your power tool. *You use the power of your attention.* You remember what you want. Remember. You have created Point A—departure and Point B—arrival. You have utilized the Law of Definition and *defined* a *Word of powerful intention.* Now you want to focus everything you have on that Word. Repeat the mantra that states your intention. Over and over again you repeat your mantra. You repeat it with enthusiasm and with passion. You are saying to the universe and to your ego, *Listen, listen, hear me, this is the existence I want, this is the beauty and intelligence, the peace and success, I truly want.* Over and over you call it, in spite of your resistance, in spite of anything you might be feeling. You call it knowing that you truly want a new existence. You tell yourself that you will not be attached to how it comes; you will trust your Spirit, your God, your place in Creation. You tell yourself to trust the process. You get on board the train and head for Point B. Imagine that your Word is an arrow winging its way straight into the heart of Creation and coming back to you as Point B.

Let go of arrogance. Of course you are arrogant, the ego is characterized by arrogance. Practice humility. Arrogance-humility is a polarity—one line. Arrogance is a refusal to receive anything you are afraid you can't control. Humility is the willingness to surrender control and receive Guidance, receive Gifts, receive the Intelligence and Beauty of God, receive your real life. Receive what is truly yours. Use your spiritual practices and take these practices seriously and *personally.* Very few people take their spiritual practices *personally.* People tend to take their ego-derived, fear-driven reactions personally. This is the arrogance of the ego. Stop taking your ego personally.

Take your words personally; take your spiritual practices personally. Re-create your self and you create a new world. Believe it. In the humility of truth, be willing to experience your real power to create actual, magical changes in yourself and your world. *What Words do you want to take into your new life? What Words do you want to take into your next moment? What Words do you want to bring to life?*

CHOICE: YOUR AGREEMENT WITH GOD

I want to say something about that word "choice" since I advise you to use it when you create your mantras. I suggest that you use the phrase "I Choose To Receive ____" when you create your mantras.

"Choice" is a word that represents your intentions. Whether those intentions are conscious or unconscious, they are choices. "Choice" is a word that has become a spiritual cliché. A cliché comes into being because what it describes or defines is true. It is true that conscious choice is powerful. But with the New Age ideology the word has become emotionally and psychologically loaded with false significance. In this false ideology, everything is about choice, and students become afraid they will be punished if they don't make the right choice—like, you will get an F if you don't have the right answer, and if the choice you make is the right answer, it is proof that you are good at manifesting impressive forms. The potential for failure here is just as bad as in any other ideology of egocentric and unreal expectations. Since the ideology states that everything is a choice, then every bad thing that happens contains the potential for blame and "it's your *choice*" can easily become "its your *fault*". The ideology of choice is even used as an excuse for judging or condemning others. "Why should I help you, you *chose* it!" The word "choice" is as overused and misused as the word "karma".

In teaching, I use the word "choice" to signify your agreement with God—or you could say if you like, your agreement with your own Essential Self, with Creation itself. This agreement states your willingness to receive. You are telling Creation that you are open and willing to surrender your ego, your pain, confusion, and anger, and that you are willing to offer your mind and heart, your hands and your voice, for the sake of Truth, for peace, for compassion, for the sake of your most passionate dream of freedom and abundance.

Receiving is an art. Religious culture does not teach us to receive. We are taught that it is blessed to give and selfish to receive. So we have, as a species, learned to fear lack; we panic at the thought of doing without, of lacking the means to survive; and this has taught us to self-righteously take. And at the same time we are punished for taking, for being selfish. We are taught the *survival of the fittest* along with *blessed are the meek.* And our judgments of who is fittest are based on some very superficial images and beliefs. We are taught to manipulate greed. We are taught ways and means of self-importance. But we are not taught that receiving is blessed. This way of thought has created the deep and toxic guilt that haunts our planet and haunts our dreams.

It is astonishing how much energy we spend keeping ourselves from receiving. We argue with God believing we are too unworthy to receive treasure. We condemn and envy rich people. We actually fear abundance and receiving because somewhere—probably in the concept of original sin, which made human guilt a cosmic agreement and travail and suffering a fit punishment from God for our base and sinful nature—we took on the notion that we aren't supposed to joyously receive. Can we really believe in an unconditionally loving deity and say that this deity wants us to suffer because we are inherently sinful? It's a lie.

In this case, the choices you make do not matter so much as the action of making a choice. In the action of choosing deliberately, you are making an agreement to co-create, to honor the life force, to honor human creativity. In the action of making your choices a conscious action, you are saying to Creation "I am willing to be accountable for myself. I am willing to receive and honor Life." You are saying to God, "Give me What I Am". *I am willing.*

Grace is a gift that doesn't have to be paid for in suffering. Grace is a filling that happens when you are empty of expectations. When you have no more expectations, you are open to receive and you are filled. Grace fills you and you give of yourself simply, easily, without thought and without conditions. Receiving and giving are one smooth motion. A circulation of blessing. One divine state of being.

Choose to receive and embody human grace and live your life in a way that transmutes all the conditions you have placed in your own path. Choose to receive blessing for yourself and you will continuously pour out blessing into the lives of all beings you will meet on your path. In this way you give from a full heart. If you are receiving, you are full. If you are full and keep receiving, you overflow. So for the sake of all beings who do not know how loved they are, choose to receive a life of human grace. Choose to be willing to receive blessings with no conditions. Remember humility means the willingness to receive. Arrogance is an attempt to control what you receive. The blessings that come from your willingness are gifts that circulate and grow in you and expand out to others. Keep this blessing moving.

CHAPTER 6

THE PRINCIPLE OF POLARITY

To destroy an undesirable rate of mental vibration, put in operation the Principle of Polarity and concentrate upon the opposite pole to that which you desire to suppress.

The Kybalion

HEAT AND COLD constitute a polarity. Can you tell on a thermometer where cold ends and heat begins? East and west constitute a polarity. If you travel far enough west you reach the far east. If you keep going east you reach west. Polarities are opposite poles on the same line separated only by degrees. They are not absolutes. They are opposite intentions but not opposite in any absolute either-or sense. They vibrate on the same energy line. It is always possible to transmute the energy of a polarity. The vibration of hate can be transmuted to the vibration of love. *The Art of Polarization is a phase of Mental Alchemy known and practiced by ancient and modern Hermetic Masters. An understanding of the Principle will enable one to change his own Polarity, as well as other polarities, if he will devote the time and study necessary to master the art. (The Kybalion)*

Polarizing a problem allows you to think in a new way about obstacles and challenges because it changes your relationship to the problem. Polarity as it is utilized in esoteric traditions, and as I use it in the Course, represents Dr. Martin Luther King's *creative tension*. Dr King defined creative tension as the harmonic *polarity* of stress. He defined it as the tension necessary for a dream to take shape and become real. He also defined it as an energy that fills you with faith, an energy that comes into being when you refuse to be a victim, choose to overcome, and keep your eye on the prize. Creative tension is a perfect harmony that resolves itself into a new creation. I once heard a preacher define creative tension as God *stretching the cord*, stretching the energy of Creation to create room for something new. Utilizing the principle of polarity gives you a new relationship with tension.

"Tension" is usually defined as stress and tension as stress is confining, constricting; it squeezes; it is painful, and it goes nowhere. All that this kind of tension can do is create more stress. Creative tension is fluid, perfectly balanced, perfectly timed—imagine the symmetry of bird wings. Creative tension is Divine Order in action. In perfect rhythm it hums through the air around you and energizes all your most powerful dreams. Creative tension is an outcome of the principle of polarity.

How does polarity work as a Hermetic principle? It works on the esoteric principle of Vibration. It is not necessary to know vibration in order to utilize the principle of polarity. Measuring the frequency of vibration is a way of measuring energy. It provides a scale of proportion. For example, if energy vibrates on a scale of one to ten, the physical realm would be vibrating at a one and the Christ Consciousness would be vibrating at a ten and in-between would be the Astral body (*emotional body*) vibrating at a five. These categories allow us to map the various energies that make up our world, it puts them into proportion. Energy is relative to itself. Point A is relative to Point B. Point B resonates a higher vibration of energy which, if you deliberately intensify and further raise the vibration, allows it to transmute Point A.

Creating a deliberate polarity allows you to visualize *separation;* it gives you a map of where you are separate from your Self. This allows your mind to directly address the separation and more easily work toward unity. To create a conscious polarity, you take the thing you want to transmute, call it lump of coal or trash, and you "name" it. Write down the name. This creates one pole of a polarity. Call it Point A. Then draw a line to the opposite pole and "name" it—name the treasure, the diamond, the definition of the thing you want to receive. Write down this name. Call it Point B.

This practice allows you to look at where you are polarized in your *intentions.* A—lump of coal and B—diamond. Practice being aware of both points while keeping your eye on Point B. Holding a visible map of your consciousness is a practice that stretches your mind. This is why I ask you to write it down. Actually create, on paper, the visible map of what you want your consciousness to do and practice stretching your attention to include both poles—simultaneously letting go of one while receiving the other.

As you learn to hold these two contradictory truths at A—B, it teaches you to be at ease with contradictions. Keep your eye on the prize but do not ignore the lump of coal. I said in chapter three that the Hermetic teachings warn against misunderstanding the principle of polarity—beware of omitting *either side* of the paradox. Be honest about your departure (Do you like the way you are?) and be honest about where you want to arrive. (What do you want?). You accept both realities knowing that you are calling into being a greater reality that is truer than either Point A or Point B. In the laws of magic this is called the Law of Synthesis wherein two contradictory truths can be held in place and used to create a third truth that is even more true. In the third truth, all contradictions are resolved and what manifests is more powerful than the two original contradictory truths. This is humorously referred to as working the Law of True Falsehood. Point A and Point B are resolved in Point C. This creates what in esoteric teachings is referred to as a Triangle of Causality, a multidimensional form that contains all the possible ramifications of A and B plus the best possible result that can come from polarizing A and B. It is creative tension that allows you to hold all this energy without having to think about it.

Transformation begins with the lump of coal. When you shift your attention away from coal, *reverse* your attention to the opposite pole, and "name" diamond, you create a Word of Power. A Word of Power states your *intention.* If you have a strong intention it is like magnetic true north, it directs the needle of your focused attention.

This creates heat. Heat drives the train toward the new destination. With your attention focused on a mantra that states your intention to receive diamond, the lump of coal receives no more of your attention, and it dissolves. Your potential diamond, your Word of Power, is receiving tremendous amounts of attention; of energy—powerful heat. Therefore it takes on form, takes shape, comes into being and you have manifested a diamond. And except for a piece of interfering consciousness called "ego," it really is that simple.

A—departure—<creative tension>—B—arrival = C—new form. The new creation allows contradictions to dissolve. Creation takes any discrepancy and turns it into a new arrival, a new form. And each new arrival creates the unfolding of a new beginning, and you reach toward greater truth. God stretches the cord to make room for a new existence. Creation comes up with an equivalent Word and a new beginning. Creation never stops. It unfolds. Point B is always a new beginning.

Opposite poles are powerful *because* they are opposite poles. It is possible to create a powerful energy between opposite poles if you approach each pole in a consciously focused way. Why is that? If your attention is focused only on one pole, point A, your thoughts and emotions will be fixated there with only one possibility. You will create more point A existence You run a constant commentary to yourself describing the lack and despair, anger, or whatever feelings you feel about yourself and your existence. You run constant memos to yourself about what is wrong, who to blame and how to fix it—your energy loops round and round accumulating more and more energy at point A. Within this fixed energy loop, change cannot happen because your fixed attention is a strong focus that keeps energizing the problems at Point A. This is the ego loop. A fixed thought form created from old *definitions* of reality.

Likewise if you are longing for change but never state a strong intention to let go of where you are at and an equally strong intention to receive a new existence, the longing remains vague, impotent, and unfulfilled. You do not have a powerful Point B. You talk to yourself about the things you long for but simultaneously talk about why you can't have them. The energy has no direction, nowhere to go, and it dribbles away into anxieties that reinforce self-pity, feed your victim, reinforce the ego loop, and create a frustrated existence.

Whereas, if you can simply define the sense of lack or the problem in your life with no commentary—and simultaneously define and declare a strong intention to receive a new existence, your old existence can be released and your new existence can manifest. You have a polarity map. A map of your actual existence without the commentary. It is the constant commentary that gives life to your old existence. If you stop sending memos to yourself about your wounded self, your victim, your *if only* and *yes, but* list, and just name Point A as it is, you will have a departure point. Once you have a departure, you have a chance to arrive at a new existence by defining it (also with no commentary) at Point B. Don't write any memos to yourself about Point B. By approaching both poles energetically, you create the immense energy that is needed to change lack into treasure. It is very easy to create tremendous amounts of energy—you simply utilize your attention in new and powerful ways by using the art of polarization.

ESSAY ON CREATIVE TENSION FROM THE REAL MAGIC COURSE:

In the technology of magic, the "*How*" does not matter, only the "*What*" matters.

I once had an art history teacher who described Picasso as having taken the "how" and put the "what" with it. That stayed with me for years and sorting out what my teacher meant by that assisted in the evolution of my philosophy of life and my understanding of polarity and led to an understanding of the necessity for structure when working with art or alchemy.

There are two contradictory forces in human consciousness—ego and Spirit. These forces have created two kinds of human thought process—two ways of thinking. Lets call them mental, linear thinking and creative, magical thinking. Each of these ways of processing your thoughts creates *tension.*

Tension is polarized energy—it does not have to be stressful. A stress oriented, linear, emotionally charged mental process is often characterized by conflict, anxiety about contradictions, feeling powerless, or feeling victimized. Stress oriented thinking is focused on control, focused on how to fix stress and be *in control* again. It goes round and round in an ego loop. This focus is centered in the belief that if you can control "how;" the *ways and means* by which a desired outcome can come into being, you can control the outcome and you will not have to deal with any nasty surprises. This thought process requires constant focusing on the *process*. A lot of contradictions can appear when you are focused on controlling your process. If you want to practice Real Magic, you learn to let go of controlling the process. Control of the process is only important if you are baking a cake.

When you are bent on controlling how to create a particular outcome, contradictions will arise. These contradictions can appear to be dangerous, and much of your creative energy gets tied up in trying to prevent or fix contradictions—make them a solid either/or. This comes from the mistaken belief that if you can make those contradictions go away, your confusion will be fixed and you will get the outcome you want. Focusing on how to make things happen so that you will get the outcome you want keeps you in the ego loop, processing the ways in which you can control your process. Real Magic axiom, "Don't Process Your Process."

This focus on process can keep you in a state of constant anxiety about outcomes and constant second-guessing. This discourages any outcome except stress, and since stress begets stress, it makes you a little crazy—actually it can make you very crazy to be continually beset by contradictions that can't get fixed and won't go away! Every artist knows that accidents are part of the creative process and if you let go of trying to fix a "mistake," that mistake becomes part of the process and often leads to the creation of something better than you had imagined. You cannot improvise jazz unless you are willing to be inspired by "mistakes" and let the mistake move you into a greater creation. Creating requires you to trust Creation and let go of the "how" and let go of anxiety about outcomes. Don't be afraid of mistakes and contradictions.

Letting go of process enables you to create the tension that exists in magical thinking. If I keep mentioning creative tension it is because repetition is powerful, and trusting creative tension is an important factor in manifesting. Creative tension is not new. Da Vinci knew it, and many poets, painters, writers, musicians, and spiritual visionaries have acknowledged it. Dr. King mentioned creative tension often as an energy that happens when you let go of "I can't" and begin your walk one step at a time toward the prize.

Creative tension is dynamic, moving moment to moment to evolve an orderly process of creative rhythm that resolves all contradictions without stress. This happens when you let go of process and, at the same time, trust the process. Everything is taken care of in creative trust. Creative tension is an energy that moves naturally in synchronicity with the most powerful available energy. You create available energy by focusing on your mantras, letting go of the old and focusing attention on the new. Creative tension is Divine Order; it will strengthen your intention and help keep your attention easily focused. Practice getting the *feel* of the difference between creative tension and stress.

In magic the What creates the How—that's why it is magic. What does this mean? *How* refers to process. *What* refers to your intention. If your attention is focused on *How* to get the *What* to happen, you are focused on process. In reality, you do not have to do anything with process. Life is in process all the time; process just means movement toward something. If your point A is stress, and you are too focused on process, you might find yourself always manifesting and processing stress. If you keep letting go of *How* to get the *What* and simply focus *on* the What, the How naturally creates its own movement. If the What is clear, the How is effortless and the result is powerful.

When I was a very young jazz vocalist, just a baby really, I was afraid to scat. In those days—that was long, long ago—musicians were very scornful of vocalists who tried to make horn sounds. My phrasing was good and I had a friend who encouraged me to try scatting as a way to loosen up my sound. He told me that no one could tell me how, that the *how* had to take care of itself, he said to just drop myself into the sound anywhere, that there was no right place to begin, and to do it as if I didn't give a damn, to just close my eyes and let the sound carry me where it wanted to go and all I had to do was follow the rhythm and breathe. He was describing the creative process. And I have remembered his words every time I began something new, whether it was trying a new recipe, a piece of sculpture, or creating a class. It is all a creative process and if you trust Creation and keep letting go of how to do it, the process moves simply toward a perfect outcome. And you will experience a rose that blooms where no rose was planted. Creation will surprise you.

I have had people take exception to this, thinking I am talking about some kind of New Age nirvana where everyone just stays mellow and does their thing and no one has to make any effort, or bother to learn a craft. Not so. When I say "the how" I am not talking about craft. Craft—the tools, the technology, your practices—is the foundation upon which you build your life. Remember the parable Jesus told about a house built on sand and a house built on rock? Mastery is a house built on rock. Practice your brush strokes, your violin, your vocalizing, your spiritual practices, because they lead you to the grace that comes when the craft is forgotten and you are the choiceless choice, the effortless stroke, the sound that drops perfectly into the perfect interval. Craft is about mastery. Mastery just plain feels good—strong, grounded, and confident in your Self. Without the skeleton, the muscles have no anchor. Without foundation the house will fall in the first high wind. Learn your craft. Practice, practice, practice. Craft is *not about process*. Craft is about unfoldment. Craft is about being. Let go of process but learn your craft!

Contradictions and conflicts aren't important and can easily change to serene understanding. Be at ease with contradiction and create the *What* that matters most to you. As you move into a creative way of looking at your life, every challenge in your ongoing life is met with a lift into creative tension and rather than immediate fear or defensiveness, you feel *interested.* Interested in what you can create in response to whatever the challenge may be. As you practice trusting the process, you learn to trust that Creation can create a better "How" than you can. Keep letting go of process and keep your eye on your Intention. Name any quality—freedom, truth, peace, grace—that you truly want and choose to receive it. It will manifest.

Because you can. Beyond beliefs, beyond contradictions, beyond any known process, you can have your real life because that is what you are here for. And as we learn to create from purpose and not from need, trusting that there is enough, as we let go of our species fear of lack, we create a society based on trust. Imagine what the world could be like if we were not motivated by fear of lack? If we were motivated by the understanding that there is always enough. This is what Jesus meant by the "lilies of the field". He did not mean stop working and creating, inventing and producing. He meant live with no fear of lack. He meant use what we know to support life and the life force, to support Creation. He did not mean that we stop receiving challenges to our creativity. He meant that we are creators and if we live in love with Creation, God will love with us. Love is a co-creation. Choose to receive life, and life will grace you. That's what He meant.

CHAPTER 7

POWER POINTS:

LIVING IN THE VITAL MOMENT

THERE IS NO such thing as being *in the moment.* As soon as you think about the moment, it is gone, and you are in the next moment and the next. At the same time, you are *always* in the moment; you can't *not* be in the moment. So what spiritual teachers mean when they say be "in the moment" has to do with awareness—with being conscious at all times. Being in the moment has to do with your *attention.* The power point practice is a practice of bringing your conscious *attention* into your moments of stress. The power point practice teaches you to use the power of your Attention to bring clarity and discernment into moments of intense stress. In a stressful moment you are overwhelmed by emotionally heightened reactions. If you can learn to turn moments of heightened stress into moments of heightened awareness you can easily make any change in yourself you want to make at the moment when the change is most desired.

Taking the energy of your most emotionally intense, out of control moments and utilizing that energy in behalf of your truth is the key to transmuting energy. This practice of "pointing" power in the direction you want it to go—i.e. from fear into faith or from frustration into peace—in the vital moment when you are most strongly feeling the fear or frustration, leads to mastery. This practice allows you to powerfully transmute energy in the moment. Power point practice helps you break your ego's habitual loop into the past, into stress, or into false and potentially dire outcomes.

When I first started teaching, every moment was potentially stressful. I was projecting so much fear of what might happen and I was trapped in the belief that I had to be perfect if I was going to teach. I believed that if I wasn't perfect I could ruin someone's life. I became more and more afraid of losing control. I was clumsy and often clueless because I was not allowing myself to be present with what was actually happening. So I made an agreement with myself that I did not have to be perfect or even know how to be a "good" teacher. That all I needed was willingness to *be* a teacher. I practiced moments of stress or challenge as moments of heightened awareness and taught myself that in those moments it was all right to stop and do something to shift the energy I was in—not get trapped in the moment. I had hypnotized myself into believing I had to be in control all the time and letting myself know that I didn't have to be in control; that I could make mistakes and not damage anyone was a major shift in my consciousness. I would let myself stop and pray—and sometimes I would include my students in that moment. I would tell them I had to stop because I was afraid my fear was teaching the class, or my arrogant fear of being wrong was teaching the class, or my fear of their pain was teaching the class—my ego was teaching the class. I came to realize—because they informed me—that this was an important learning for them. That my stopping and dropping my ego right in front of them made the practice of letting go of ego much more available to them because it took the fear out of it. I was breaking the ego loop for all of them.

My first classes were disastrous. It seems very humorous now, a comedy of errors filled with wonderful redeeming moments. I learned from my disasters how to define and use what I now teach as power points. I began by calling those moments of stress and paralysis moments of *not-knowing*, and I practiced being careful to catch those moments and shift the energy into *knowing*. Then I learned the esoteric meaning of vital moments and began to shift these moments of not-knowing by calling them vital moments. And vital moments evolved to become power points. Utilizing these moments in a deliberate way breaks the ego loop. It interrupts your ego, stops it in its tracks. This practice makes you smarter because it clears the way to your own deeper, higher, more intelligent resources in the moment.

ESSAY ON POWER POINTS FROM THE REAL MAGIC COURSE

What do I mean by "power point?" A power point is a moment of extreme emotional stress. In a power point your senses are expanded and you are overwhelmed, impacted by an event, by a person, by any catalyst that is activating stress and causing intense disappointment, intense anger, intense *feelings.* You are lost in the emotion of the moment and you, in that moment, aren't concerned with change; you don't even *want* to change. Flight or fight—you want to run and hide or fight and destroy. You want to be in control. You want to be safe according to all your ego definitions of what control and safe mean. You feel victimized and defensive. Overwhelmed by your victim feelings, you believe that victim is truth. Overwhelmed by anger, you believe that anger is truth. Overwhelmed by despair, you believe that despair is truth. You are self-righteous. You are full of self-importance.

Your deepest beliefs come up in your moments of intense stress because these moments are *primal* and they energize your deepest hopes and fears. In that moment, the only thing you obey and trust is the emotion you are feeling. You believe that your feelings don't lie and can be trusted to tell you what is real in that moment. Your feelings feel real. Your disappointment, anger, pain, humiliation, feels real to you. But *is* it real? Can your feelings be trusted? Does that feeling you are feeling constitute the state of being you *actually* want in that moment? Does it constitute the existence you truly want? Is anger the word you want to take into your next moment? Is victim the word you want to take into your next moment?

You can use that moment of intense stress as a chance to turn your whole existence around. The concept of using stress points powerfully is not new, particularly in the esoteric traditions where a student is in training to master emotional states. In esoteric teachings, adepts are trained to view moments of overwhelming stress as *vital moments.* The training consists of methods for turning the energy of that stress point around and making it work for you rather than against you. Students are taught that in vital moments they can utilize the magical *Law of Reversal* to increase the power of their intentions. The Law of Reversal comes into play when you recognize that you are in a power point and *reverse the direction of your attention.* You can create a tremendous energy shift if you, in the moment, shift the direction of your attention away from old fixed attention (Point A) to a *more* powerful *conscious* intention (Point B). Don Juan calls power points "points of Intent" when the Intention of Spirit can powerfully manifest.

What happens if you define this moment of overwhelming stress as a moment of vital power that can be used to your advantage? What happens if you can realize that, as intense as they might be, your feelings in that moment are not what matters? If you can force yourself to realize, at that moment, that the deliberate choice you make is more important than the feeling you are feeling, then real magic can happen. When you are in a vital moment, a power point, your power to deliberate, to notice *what is* and make clear choices is the only power that matters.

So—a power point is a moment of intense stress when you are facing a challenge and are overwhelmed by feelings of anger, fear, hopelessness, fatigue, self-righteousness, self-pity, etc. You might feel powerless to control the situation—yet you feel compelled to control the situation. Your ego has one goal, safety. To be safe means you *have* to be *right* because you can only control the energy of your environment if you are *right.* Ego loop. The human ego is terrified of being wrong. *(And if you stop and think on the many centuries of being misnurtured and unnurtured, manipulated and pushed around that the human being has experienced, then you will be compassionate toward yourself and your species.)* Cultivate patience and let go of any fear of being wrong. This breaks the loop.

In those moments of stress you will react according to your old emotional patterns. Since human beings are taught from birth to *manipulate* energy and control *survival*, you will fall back on that ability to manipulate when you are stressed. Usually these moments are triggered by other people and can instantly become power struggles. What can you do? First of all, manipulation is futile because it creates karma. When you are manipulating energy you are trying to control another person's choices so that you will be safe. What can you do that is not manipulation? To begin with, you can shift your attention away from the notion that your stress is about other people. As long as you can believe stress is about someone else, you can blame someone else. Your stress is about you. Start with that. Everything in that moment is yours to create. What do you want?

A time of intense stress is the time to practice power points. If you are utilizing the power point training you will, at the first sign of stress, immediately reverse your attention, *shift poles* from point A to point B. And *let go*—let go of control, let go of judgments and assumptions, let go of outcomes, and *reverse*—shift into the energy of your powerful, deliberate, conscious attention. Turn it away from the stress, anger, fear, anguish and toward new and powerful intentions. *This is alchemy. You apply the Fire of God to the energy of that moment. And all the emotional intensity turns in the direction of your truth.*

Utilizing power points takes practice. It can take years to master these energies. It can take weeks or months of practice before you easily remember that when you are most stressed, you are in a power point and you can do something powerful for yourself *without harming anyone or anything*. In stress, your attention is in an old fixed place that feels familiar and right and your ego is telling you that you have to get your world under control. And in order to know you are in control, everyone involved has to admit that you are right. When you are caught up in the energy of a vital moment, everyone involved in that moment becomes a potentially dangerous other. You are on accelerated ego-power and you have to be right. A very powerful choice that you can make every day that will assist you in power points is to choose to let go of your fear of being wrong. The most powerful thing you can do in a power point is to let go of self-importance—let go of taking *anything* personally, let go of being attached to any outcome. This creates Freedom.

If you are in the power point and can't think of a mantra, just quickly think, "Point B" and the action of that mental shift will key you into remembering what it is you actually want in that moment. Any mantra is good in a power point because what is important in that moment is the action of noticing that moment of power *when you are in it.*

A power point is an opportunity for mastery. You are teaching yourself to recognize that *deliberation,* deliberate choice and conscious attention, is more powerful than your old, fixed, attention. When you first begin your practices, you will likely remember that you were in a power point after the fact—later, when the energy has subsided and you are thinking of all the crushing and victorious things you wish you had done or said. This might happen when you are home in bed trying to sleep, obsessing about what happened and who said what and who is to blame and how to fix it, and you suddenly realize that you were in a power point. Don't worry. And do not condemn yourself. Treat it then and there as a power point because the truth is that you are still in it—you are still living in and attached to that moment of stress. Take the stress, reverse your attention, and choose to receive a new intention. Stress is obstructed creativity. The polarity of stress is creative tension and even practicing your power points after the fact will increase your connection with creative tension.

Power point training teaches you to be present in each moment of your existence. Practicing power points teaches you to live in the moment without thinking of being in the moment. It frees you from thinking about what being in the moment means, from making a project of being in the moment, or believing that you have to be in the moment in order to be spiritual. Practicing power points moves you into just *being*—totally present in the moments of your life. It teaches you that the "moment" is wherever you are at, and deliberately choosing your moments brings you to a state of always knowing where you are at. Being in the moment means knowing where you are at in each moment. And *enjoying* where you are at. Whether you are imagining beauty in a beautiful dream, painting a picture, cleaning out your garage, fixing your lawn mower, making love, baking a cake, making a difficult decision, or meeting a conflict of interests, you are present. You are not worrying about whether you are in the moment because you *know* you are present. A power point is a point where you master your ability to take appropriate creative spiritual action immediately, concurrent with the event and not hours, days, or years after the event. This is mastery. Choose to master the vital moment.

CHAPTER 8

CREATING A PERSONAL SACRED GEOMETRY

THIS CHAPTER IS about Self-Creation. In esoteric systems, Self-Creation—to re-create yourself in the image of truth, is the highest form of transformation and the highest homage you can pay to Spirit. Self-Creation is based on the principle that you yourself are the polarity that you are transmuting. Your polarity is self (ego, matter) and Self (Soul, Spirit). This transformation utilizes the same tools you would use to transmute any form of energy. These tools are the principle of polarity and the Law of Definition. In the esoteric tradition of Self-Creation the human being is looked at as a creative matrix, a creative energy vortex, with the possibility of creating from a distorted geometry or a divine proportion. Always we are choosing.

In the esoteric traditions using the principle of polarity to structure thought enables you to create a structure of energy called a Triangle of Causation. A triangle is a sacred space, a creative matrix based on the principle of opposite poles being capable of holding intense, focalized creative energy. This creates a structure within which organizing energies can converge and be contained and directed toward a particular and ongoing intention.

Understanding these two primary spiritual tools, The principle of polarity and The Law of Definition, allows you to create energy structures of conscious intention that are like magic mirrors reflecting a universe of constant wisdom, beauty, and truth. This creates a life that is a magical anything-box, a life that is equivalent to a constant, personal, sacred geometry, a matrix within which the whole structure of life can become a safe and sacred, creative adventure.

Imagine that your physical body and your subtle energy body equal one large creative matrix. You are a vortex of energy that holds tremendous creative potential. Using Polarity and Definition you can create anything that you can imagine *within your own creative matrix.* Being a personal creative matrix that is part of a vast, limitless creative universe, allows you the free will to create a life of beauty and richness. Artists have an inherent knowing that life is a creative matrix within which it is only necessary to imagine life, and Creation, the Sophia, the Vast Wisdom Matrix, will provide the Way, the *how* that can bring the imagined *what*, your real life, into physical being.

Whatever your beliefs, whether you think life is about quantum physics or TV evangelism, you are participating in a great matrix of imagined forms, of imagined social and religious ideals, and you are creating yourself within this vast world. You are a work of art that is continually in process.

Our artists and our musical and poetic messengers have testified for centuries that life is a constantly moving, universal creative process. Your own Soul is constantly calling forth the artist, the creator within you. What do you imagine the vast Soul of Creation has been trying to teach us? It is time to de-mystify magic, to de-mystify art and learn what Creation really is. It is time to de-mystify mystery and experience true Mystery.

How can we experience true Mystery? Let your Soul lead you. What enchants your life? Live it. Not as a fantasy, fantasizing to compensate for what you think you lack. And not as settling for less in order to feel safe. Life is not a matter of being pragmatic and settling for less, adapting to lack while at the same time using fantasy to distract yourself from your pain, or using fantasy to help you maintain the illusion of satisfaction within a marginal existence. Being true to yourself means being true to God and being true to God means living life full-out. This does not mean live irresponsibly. It means live with true personal accountability, with self-knowledge.

Live life as vision, as a work of art, as Real Magic. De-mystify the creative process, and see it as something all humans do and something that all human beings can learn to do consciously. Take charge of your own creative process and create your masterpiece.

Live life as a *What,* not as a *How.* Life is awareness. Life is listening. Life is questing. What can I create next? What do I want the world to be? What Word do I want to bring to life in my matrix? What is it that defines my true Soul, my true world? Love? *Choose* it. Nurturing? Choose it. No more frightened, terrorized, battered, hungry, starving, un-nurtured, mis-nurtured, people? Choose it. Choose to live your profound, enchanted, true, life.

How? Apply the principle of polarity to yourself. Make of yourself a polarity map of self and Self. A Triangle of Causation. Imagine yourself as a matrix vortex, holding the energy of new existence. Do you want to create a sacred existence for yourself? Use the principle of polarity and the Law of Definition. The way that you *define* your existence is vital. The way you call it is the way that it will manifest. All present experience, whether it be failure or success, comes from the way that you have *defined* yourself and your world. Your definition of yourself is the most powerful thought-sound energy you carry. The mantra that keeps your present thought-sound-form intact is your given name. *The Power of the Word.* Your *given name* is a mantra that contains—as in container—the energy of your whole existence. Your whole story is written in your given name. What can you do with this information?

Re-define your existence. Write a new story. Write a story about yourself living the existence you would truly love to be living. Create a song of celebration to your Self, a praise song dedicated to what enchants your heart, what satisfies your Soul. Give this story of celebration your *name.* Use your name as a conscious mantra and a talisman. A talisman is something you wear on your person. A talisman is a kind of energy shorthand that represents a strong intention. A talisman can be a piece of jewelry that you engrave with your name, a piece of cloth that you embroider, a vial containing a scroll that you incorporate into a necklace and wear around your neck, a bead, an elaborate jewel, or a word written on a piece of paper and carried in your pocket.

In all esoteric teachings, Self-Creation is the most potent form of transformation, and these transformative, esoteric teachings are directed toward the actual transmutation of the ego. Esoteric teachings use every form of human condition as an opportunity for transformation. A primary esoteric teaching is to wear a talisman that contains *both* an image of the condition you wish to transmute (point A) *and* the desired form you wish to bring into being (point B). This is an application of the principle of polarity and the Law of Definition. As a talisman for a new existence, you would wear your own name, symbolized by a written word and also by an image. With the talisman image you wear you also use your name as a mantra, a sound you repeat. Using these tools of Polarity, Image, and Word, you can bring into being a new existence.

It is as if you take your name and magically imprint your name with the energy of a new story. Repeat the new story by using talisman and mantra until the new story vibrates to your name and begins to come true and the old story dissolves. Don't be afraid to let go of your old story. Letting go of your old story doesn't mean severance from anything you love. Anything that is truly yours remains with you. You cannot lose your Soul. Again, trust the creative process. Your Soul is in agreement with God.

At this point you are probably asking yourself if I am talking about changing your name. No. I am talking about the energy of the thing. What does the energy field of your name look like? It looks like you. The energy of your name resonates to your definition of yourself. Don't make up a new name. Use your given name, your own existing name, but change your definition of your life. *Changing* your name has no lasting power unless you *transmute the energy* of the name you have carried all your life, your given name.

What am I talking about? My name is Sylvia. Imagine that I am attempting to transform my existence. Someone studying modern day shamanism says to me that I must change my name—Sylvia—to a new magical power name. So I change my name to something exotic and evocative like Pontia Ford or Bella Dream or

Luna Rosa. Several months or years later I realize that nothing has changed except that I am stuck with a name that doesn't feel like me and has never felt like a true fit.

Why didn't the new name work to change the Sylvia existence? Because the name change did not transmute the energy of the given name Sylvia. At a deep primal level the energy in the name Sylvia is still vibrating the same old primal Sylvia. And the primal Sylvia is still manifesting the fears and resistance that Sylvia has always manifested. Whatever new name you lay on top of it, the primal energy of your given name will attach itself to the new name. And nothing will change.

Transmute your given name by changing the vibration. By changing the vibration of energy in your name you can create a major transformation of your world. Your name can vibrate to your ego or to your Soul. You decide. Your name is a Word of Power. At the sight and sound of your name every cell of your being reacts, resonates and answers to this Word that contains the energy of your present identity, and the energy of every experience that created your present identity. Your name conjures a being, a primal definition of you. It conjures a combination of coal and diamond, depending on your definition of yourself. If you are defining yourself as a victim, your name is a mantra that conjures victim—coal. If you are defining yourself as successful and happy, your name is a mantra that conjures happiness—diamond. You could truthfully say that every time you hear your name you experience a vital moment and the definition of you that is conjured by your name is renewed.

Create a new definition of your existence. Write it. Write that new definition as a story about your deliberate and true dream of a world. Write it as a world that exists now. Don't write it as a wish or a dream for the future; write it as immediate Reality. Don't say "I wish I lived by the ocean." Say instead, "I live by the ocean." Don't say, "I wish I had my own business." Say, "I have my own business." Don't say, "I wish I was." Say, "It is . . . . *and* I am." What kind of world would you like to inhabit? What existence would you give yourself if you could have any existence you could imagine? Imagine that any existence you are able to imagine is an existence that you can create. Then imagine that existence.

Be free. Be spontaneous, even outrageous in your imaginings. Don't judge your imagination; let it carry you. See this practice as a creative experiment. Give yourself time. Do a retreat and take a whole day to contemplate, meditate on, and imagine a new existence—especially imagine the quality of life, how your new existence *feels.* Imagine yourself walking in Beauty. How does that feel? What does it look like? Write it into your new story. Imagine yourself walking in peace, abundance, and freedom. How does that feel? What does it look like? Write it into your new story. Use capital letters. Imagine yourself living in The Divine Mother's Garden. What is that like? This is a beautiful exercise. Write your new story.

Imagine that you live in a house that embodies the feel of sacredness. Imagine. What is most sacred to you? What does sacred feel like? What does it look like? Imagine living in a state of creative adventure. How does that feel? What have you created that you want to celebrate? What will you bring to life in your future? Imagine yourself walking in Compassion. What does Compassion feel like? What does Compassion look like? Imagine an Eloquent life. Walk in Eloquence. What does Eloquence feel and look like? Imagine an Elegant life. What does Elegance feel and look like? Imagine a life of Integrity. What does Integrity feel and look like? Imagine walking in wealth. What does wealth feel like? What does wealth look like? Imagine Radiance. What do all these qualities look like in your life? Imagine your existence and write your story. The Story of You. A Word Portrait of You.

Imagine that your own name is a talisman and a mantra that can create the necessary energy that will bring your new existence into being. Imagine that every time you see your name or hear your name a breath of life wafts through your mind. Imagine yourself feeling uplifted and joyous at the sound of your own name. Your name is the most personal, the most creative, the most intimate and intense possession that you have. Your total definition of who you are and a description of your existence is written energetically in your name. Every time you hear your name or see it written, your identity is reinforced. It is in your own best interest to transmute any negative energies that might be invoked when your name is spoken or written. So even if you desire to change your name, first do some work to transmute the energy of your given name.

So write a love story about your life, a true story that you imagine. A story that describes a new existence for you. Write. At the top of the page write your name as the title of your story. Read your story over and over again to yourself. Read it out loud to a dear friend or to your teacher. Read it ceremoniously so as to imprint it into your subconscious. Tell yourself that the sound of your name now conjures a new existence, that your name is now the energy of a bright promise, beautiful and true. Light candles, play your favorite music, sit before a mirror, and read your new story about yourself to yourself. Practice saying your name to yourself often, especially in times of stress, in power points. Create a talisman that uses your name. This can be as simple as writing your name on a piece of paper each day and carrying it in your pocket. Or this can be an elaborate and symbolic representation of your new life worn as a garment or jewelry, beadwork or metalwork, or even a tattoo.

When I was in Africa I observed a Holy Woman create medicine for a woman who was going through a painful divorce. She created what she called a "conjure pot" and said it was big medicine. What she did essentially was ask the woman questions about what life she would like to be having right now. Beginning with the woman's name she created representative symbols from pieces of cloth, beads, shells, bone, earth, rock, hair, blood, an ancient pallet for an ancient art. Each object represented the woman's name, and each object was imbued with the energy of *blessing a new existence*. This healer placed each object in a clay pot, sealed a lid on the pot and gave it to the woman as a conjure pot. The woman was to hold the pot each day and say her own name several times while "holding" in her hands the pot that contained the energy of her new existence. She was told to say her name often during the day and think of her conjure pot every time she said her name. So the woman's name became a mantra, a focal point of a matrix that resonated a new existence every time she said her own name or heard someone else say it.

This was the most creative ceremony I have ever seen. Every movement was created to focus the woman's attention on her new existence. It gave her mind and imagination something creative to do and that creative focus allowed the energy of the past and of the divorce to dissipate. It was utterly beautiful. I felt such gratitude that the ancient teachings I was trying so hard to incorporate into my life here in the United States were known and being used by a medicine woman on the other side of the world.

In my teaching I call the conjure pot a "Blessing Pot" and I offer it as a beautiful and effective ceremony of self-creation and self-blessing. Create a simple ceremony about writing your new self-definition, read it several times to yourself, and keep it in your Blessing Pot. Your Blessing Pot represents your creative matrix within a greater Creative Matrix. Do a simple ceremony with your name such as—remembering that your name is a mantra, write your name every day on paper and put the piece of paper in your Blessing Pot. Every time you say your name to yourself, imagine that your new existence is safe and gathering energy in your Blessing Pot.

When the Blessing Pot fills up with paper mantras, dispose of the papers by burning them and giving the ashes to the earth in some way. Don't go back and re-read your pieces of paper. Do the ceremony, then let go of being attached to your mantras or to the ceremony and go about your day. When you hit a power point in your day, say your name and feel the ceremony come to life in you—or you can envision your Blessing Pot and see yourself held safe in the arms of Creation.

You can do this Blessing Pot with all your mantras. It offers a simple and beautiful way to use an altar every day. Keep your Blessing Pot on your altar and each day write your mantras on pieces of paper and place them in your Blessing Pot. The Blessing Pot does not have to be consecrated by a religious authority. It only has to be beautiful in your eyes because it represents for you the Beauty of Creation. Imagine that your mantras are safe and gathering energy in the Cauldron of Creation or the Mother Matrix, or in God's hands. Imagine that your Blessing Pot is being held in loving hands and watched over by Beings of Loving Grace.

It is a very good idea to have an altar. It gives you a focal point and a place apart where you can be fully attentive. As you use your altar a vortex of energy comes into being around this focal point. This altar vortex is a creative matrix, a sacred space. There is no right or wrong way to work with your altar or create a ceremony. The only thing required in the creation of a ceremony is an intention. The props—altar, candles, music, photos, images, incense—are simply techniques that help you create a strong focused attention. Create an altar and ceremonies that resonate with your heart and Soul.

Keep your altar and any ceremonies you create simple and direct. Keep your words and images precise and concise. Don't get too ritualistic or symbolic or your true intention will get lost in melodrama. If you are making real magic you don't want to be distracted. You want all your faculties awake and aware and this *requires* simplicity. You don't need elaborate rituals and ceremonies. Magic works because energy does things. Whether you call it angels, miracles, or quantum mechanics, it works. Your work of art is real. Make it a celebration.

CHAPTER 9

CREATING A CONSCIOUS DAY—
A QUICKSTUDY

IMAGINE NOW THAT you are an adept in the Real Magic Mystery School. An adept is a serious, dedicated, student. What would your typical day be like? You are studying ancient practices in the midst of a busy, sometimes frantic, market place world. A world that is image, status, and money oriented. A world where marketing, pragmatism and wealth are valued and qualities like sensitivity and empathy are not always taken seriously and are even mocked. A world that is achievement oriented. What is your life like in this world? Is it the life you want?

Your first waking feeling might be anxiety. Your first waking thought is usually about the first order of business in your life. Your first order of business might be to get children ready for school or day care. It might be getting yourself to work on time or going early to your office to finish a report. Perhaps you have an interview with an employer or employee. Your first waking thought might be about your mortgage or how you are going to be able to pay next month's rent. Your first waking thought might be that you haven't found a job yet. Or the job you have doesn't pay enough. Sometimes you wake up anxious about the state of the world, or the state of your relationship with a significant person. You often wake up with a feeling of urgency, of business, of tasks that need doing, of decisions that must be made and of time running out. These thoughts are running through your consciousness before you are truly awake.

So first of all, as a Mystery School adept, create a spiritual practice that has to do with your first waking thought. What do you want your first waking thought to be? Create a wake-up mantra, a "my first waking thought" mantra and repeat it every night before you fall asleep until it *becomes* your first waking thought. This mantra could go something like, "I choose to wake up unafraid . . . I choose to wake up feeling refreshed, vital and enthusiastic about my life." This mantra can be as long or as short as you make it. It is yours so word it in a way that impacts you. I choose to wake up with a strong heart. Or wake up with a light heart. Or wake up to beauty, to harmony, to peace. Or wake up feeling clear and conscious, or happy. Wake up feeling alert, confident, trusting, and ready for the day ahead. Or just choose to wake up! You can make first waking thought mantras about making your life a masterpiece, a work of art.

Say your "first waking thought" mantra before you go to sleep every night. Then say it when you wake up each morning. Write it down and put it by your bed. Say it every time you think of it during the day. Change the wording for variety if you like but do not change the essential intention.

If you have a pressing engagement the next day that you feel anxious about, make a wake-up mantra about that and repeat it to yourself as you fall asleep. If you have something in your consciousness that you need to let go of, make a wake-up mantra about it. "I choose to let go of anxiety about outcomes" is a good all occasion mantra to say as you fall asleep. I choose to wake up to Freedom.

Once you are awake, turn your attention to your daily spiritual practices. A good daily practice is to choose a daily intention, a Word of Power for each particular day. This can be a single word or a whole phrase but keep it concise. If you like you may ask divine Guidance to give you an appropriate word. Ask your Spirit what Word would be best to carry with you and bring to life each day and quietly allow a word to come to you. People often get so caught up in thinking about material problems that they forget they can choose to manifest qualities. Often the word that comes to you will be a quality like patience, peace, compassion, joy, freedom, or strength. If a word isn't coming easily, you can think of a quality you feel you need, such as wisdom or inner strength or humor, and make that your Word of Power for the day.

There is no right way to do this practice. This is all yours. Students have picked words or phrases like, "no second-guessing, my romance, my new Volvo, Walk in Beauty, or cultivate patience". One of my favorites from a student years ago is, "trust profound irreverence!" Another is, "practice radiant brain-power". Do not put any conditions on your daily word. This practice should be pleasurable, even *fun.*

This is a great practice to do with children. You can help them come up with words that remind them how they would like to approach a particular problem, or a way they would like to be. This is a good way to teach them not to be afraid of challenges, that challenges are a part of life, and that what is important is not the challenge but the way they approach the challenge. Again, qualities work very well with this practice. You can help them pick a word in the morning, then, in the evening, talk with them about their experience during the day. This is a great focal point for teaching children that they do have a choice, and that being aware of their choices does help them do better in school, in relationships, with sibling problems, with inner feelings. It is great for teaching them where their strength lies. It shows them how strong they can be when they stop and think and choose the values and qualities that are most important to them. It helps them think toward what they want to bring to life and carry around with them. It helps teach them that inner strength is something they can create. It helps them learn that the essence of choice is not so much about things as it is about ways of being in the world, about inner qualities. And it helps them learn to take action based on what matters to them in the world. A conscious way of life is a life of self-knowledge and this practice gives children a head start toward self-inquiry and self-knowledge.

* * *

Transformation is accomplished through your commitment to your intentions, to your dedication to spiritual teachings and practices. Spiritual teachings are taught through repetition because repeated practice creates energy, and as you practice, the energy you create accumulates and helps you stay in conscious alignment with the life you truly want to live. I suggest that in order to create ongoing energy flow with your spiritual practices you create a daily or weekly worksheet and each morning consult your worksheet. Create your worksheet in the same way you prepare lists for other activities. Remind yourself to practice focusing, to remember power points, to create an altar, to pay attention to Words of Power, to meditate, etc. Create a time frame for yourself by studying your own energy and schedule in things like altar work and meditation at times when you are most able to be quiet and attentive. Make meditation, stillness, and rest a daily priority.

A word about power words. Some people have so many inhibiting beliefs about the word power that they avoid using it or addressing it in any way. If you find yourself afraid to say *any* word out loud to yourself, it is as an indication that you have inhibiting beliefs that are being triggered by that word. Transmute your relationship with words you fear by making them Words of Power. Give the word a capital letter and say it out loud at least once daily. If the word "power," or the word "love," or any other words are triggering a negative avoidance or fear response in you, realize that you are *already* giving that word a lot of power and you might be better off reversing the energy. Look at the words you fear or feel self-righteous about. Making these words conscious power words will release their locked-up creative energy.

* * *

In order to facilitate a daily or weekly worksheet I have created a quick study that covers the primary points in the Hermetic teachings and in the Real Magic Course. I would recommend reading this study often to keep yourself in alignment with *what* you are doing in the way of spiritual attention and *why* you are doing it. At the end of the quick study I have included a sample worksheet from the Course.

REAL MAGIC QUICKSTUDY OUTLINE

1. What is the most powerful thing you have?

Your attention. Pay attention to where your attention is. Does it reside in what matters most to you or is it focused on distracting yourself from your anxieties and problems? Are you ignoring—as in ignorance-problems and keeping your attention distracted? A focus on processing (how can I fix it?) your old existence can prevent change from happening because your attention is focused on the *process* of your transformation.

Attention is *energy.* Wherever your attention is focused, there will be tremendous amounts of energy and *energy makes things happen.*

2. What is the most powerful Force in the Universe?

The force of intention. Nothing happens until you make a purposeful commitment to an intention. Subconscious and unconscious beliefs serve as strong *unconscious* intentions. By giving focused attention to new and conscious intentions, you transmute undermining unconscious intentions.

3. Why do we use the principle of polarity?

Use this Hermetic principle to give yourself a visible map of where you have been and where you wish to be. Point A and Point B. Departure and arrival. This clarifies your intention and gives you an appropriate mantra. To create your polarity, ask yourself the two important questions—Do you like your life the way it is now? and What do you want?

4. What is a mantra and why use a mantra?

A mantra is a consciously chosen word that expresses a coherent intention. A mantra is a focal point, a tool that directs your attention continually toward your intention. As you continually direct your attention toward your intention, energy converges and creates a *creative tension* that brings a new form into existence.

5. What gets in the way of easily manifesting your new intentions?

Your attention is already fixed on old intentions that exist as beliefs deep in your subconscious and unconscious realms. These fixed beliefs define your identity and your relationship with the world. These fixed beliefs are like magnets pulling on your attention all the time. This keeps your identity from changing. When you begin to repeat a mantra that states a new intention, your ego fights to preserve the old fixed intention. This is what keeps you from easily manifesting changes.

6. What do you do about the part of your consciousness that is holding on to the old fixed attention?

Practice repetition. Constantly and consciously shift your attention away from point A and toward point B, so that powerful (because they are *focused*) new energies will converge and transmute the energy of the old, fixed attention (point A). Your ego maintains a powerful resistance to the new energy. Repetition is required, is *necessary*, in order to shift the energy of your ego in the direction of the new story, the new intention.

7. What is a power point?

A point of opportunity. A power point is a moment of *energized polarity*, characterized by intense feelings. You might feel anger or frustration, sadness or grief and you usually feel threatened. At a power point you often feel out of control, powerless to stop yourself or control the moment. You feel intense feelings that come from past experience and conclusions you have made in the past. In these moments it is important to recognize and not deny your feelings but do not give them, or the emotion you are feeling, any power. Feel the feeling but do not be attached to the feeling. The feeling is *giving you information about yourself* and often it is revealing the activity of a belief, or of an emotional attachment that is undermining your health or well-being. In a power point you have the opportunity to shift away from old, reactionary thought patterns and into a new reality—to shift poles from A to B by putting your attention on the opposite pole—*away* from the intense emotion you are feeling and toward your new intention.

Power point instructions: Let go of the old story. Call the new story. Turn moments of vital emotional energy into moments of vital creative energy.

8. What is the secret of letting go?

Outcomes. Let go of any attachment to outcomes. Let go of being anxious about or trying to manipulate outcomes. Let go of your old stories about damage and victim and wound. Let go of old congested energies. Make way for new vital energies.

9. What are the general rules of transformation through the Tao of Real Magic.

Be aware of the principle of polarity. Stay in touch with your intentions. Work with your mantras every day so that you will be aware of your intentions in your power points. Practice all the time. Don't practice only when you feel bad. Practice when you feel good. Practicing all the time creates a constant inner awareness that allows you to easily shift your attention in a power point when you feel bad. Claiming your vital moments transmutes any beliefs you might be carrying about being powerless. You are always powerful.

General rule: If you don't want it, don't feed it. When you no longer feed an identity of victim, your free and true Self will find the way home. Choose to master the moment. Keep your true intentions energized. Don't feed your old undermining intentions.

10. What are some good ways of energizing your true Intentions?

Practice your mantras as a daily meditation. A meditation does not have to be complicated. Just sit quietly, focused and still, breathe gently and evenly, paying attention to your in breaths and out breaths. Take deep, slow, even balloon breaths as if your torso is a balloon and you are slowly and gently filling it with air from the bottom up to the top all the way into your shoulders, then slowly and gently let it out top to bottom. As you sit in silence, quietly in your mind recite your mantras.

Create ceremonies that work with your mantras. A ceremony should be like a poem, a simple and precise statement of intention. Do not process ceremonies; create them. Keep them focused on mantras, and keep them small, precise, eloquent and, above all, simple. Eloquent does not mean elaborate. To create your ceremonies use an altar, use candles, music, color, fabric, photos, images, incense, flowers, beads, talismans and mantras. Make it up. An altar is a focal point and has one purpose; to focus your attention. A Blessing Pot on your altar is a good focal point for a ceremony to bless your new intentions. A Blessing Pot is a good weekly ceremony. A simple daily ceremony might be to just light a candle on your altar and recite a list of your mantras, or recite your daily power word.

Make a bulletin board with two columns Side A and Side B. You could head Side A as lumps of coal, or trash, departure, lead, old story, etc. Give Side B the heading of diamonds, or treasure, arrival, gold, new story, new existence, new intention, wild blue yonder, etc. Be playful and serious. Side A—cold, dark swamp and side B—tropical beach at sunset. At Side A, you want to inspire yourself to let go. And at Side B, you want to inspire yourself to receive. Make a map. Put it on the wall so that you will see it when you first wake up in the morning.

Create a collage of inspiration to place on your wall or altar. Create talismans for your altar that match talismans you can wear on your person. Use your name in a talisman that represents a new existence. If you are musical write a song to your Self. If poetic, write a poem in praise of your Spirit. Make a cartoon about your ego-self looking for a home and finding a brave new world. Paint a picture.

This is your life. Make it a work of art, a masterpiece. It is yours, so it might as well be full of wonder and congruent with the Intelligence and Beauty of God.

* * *

SAMPLE WORK SHEET FROM THE REAL MAGIC COURSE

This Course is Alchemy—learning how to use energy to change energy. This Course is not about beliefs or theories, it is about energy. We are concerned with what works, with how things happen. It is not ideas and beliefs that make things happen—energy makes things happen.

You don't have to believe these ideas in order to create focused energy; you create focused energy by focusing attention on intention.

Doing your practices creates a lot of energy. Don't waste it. This is the energy that creates change. You create change by doing the practices, not by analyzing the material in an attempt to understand the practices. So don't try to make sense of the Hermetic teachings; just do the practices. Just do it. This requires radical trust. Practice radical trust.

The worst thing your ego does to you is make you believe in separation, make you believe that you are different from others. There is no separation. Separation is not real. But this belief in separation and the belief that separation keeps you safe creates massive distrust in people. If you believe you are different from your fellow human beings you will project onto them all your fears and judgments. Then you will receive back from them hallucination in the form of your own projected fears and judgments. The worst spiritual practice you can do is compare yourself to others. If you have an image of yourself that includes inferiority, a deep fear of being wrong, you will judge others in the class as doing it better than you, as being more advanced, as being smarter than you—or you might reverse that and judge them as inferior, as not "getting it." Either way you are pitting yourself against the best in yourself. No one else has to get it.

Both of these reactions—feeling inferior or superior—are the same reaction. This is the arrogance of the ego that keeps you separate from truth, separate from your own brightest potential. This is the Catch-22 of self-importance; it keeps you second-guessing yourself. Don't do that in these classes. As you come in, consciously drop your ego at the door and do not take anything that happens in each class personally. Choose to participate fully in your own freedom. I repeat, practice radical trust.

WEEKLY PRACTICES

FOCUSING YOUR ATTENTION: Every day do a Focusing Practice. Practice making up ways to practice focus. Can you focus on two things at once? Try focusing on an object around you or on a part of your body while carrying on a conversation.

Simple Focusing Practice: Sit comfortably in a place where you have some space around you. Get very still, quietly and gently tell yourself to be still, stay still. Choose a quality such as peace, balance, or stillness. For example let us use Peace. Gently and evenly begin to breathe this quality. Peace . . . peace. Do this for several deep, slow, even breaths.

Look straight ahead and with your eyes open, and without moving your head, look up. Turn your eyes up without moving your head. Stop and say your mantra—"peace." Then turn your eyes straight ahead again.

Now look down. Again do not move your head, just your eyes. As far down as you can look. Stop and say your mantra—"peace."

Again slowly bring your eyes straight ahead. Take a deep breath, relax, and again repeat your mantra—"peace."

Now, you can stop there or continue here in an expanded focusing and energizing practice:

Now close your eyes and imagine that you are able to move your attention in the same way that you can move your eyes. And also imagine that you can move your attention as if you are reaching with your index finger and touching things with your attention.

Keep eyes closed. And focus your attention at the top of your head. Balance your focus and stay focused for several seconds at the top of your head. Take as long as you like. There is no time limit or time frame. You might experience tingling or some form of energy movement at the top of your head. This is normal.

Now focus your attention on the back of your head at the lower part, just above the hollow where the neck and skull connect. Yogananda called this a vital point, the seat of the medulla, the place where God's voice connects to the human energy field.

Keep your eyes closed as you bring your attention into balance at the back of your head. Hold it there for a few moments.

Continue with closed eyes to expand your attention and focus about two feet in front of your face. Balance your attention and hold it there for a moment, however long you like.

Then focus and expand your attention a foot or two behind your back. Balance and hold.

Then—keep eyes closed—focus one or two feet below your chair or beneath the floor if you are seated on the floor or ground. Balance and hold.

Then about one to two feet in front of your body. Balance and hold.

Now expand your attention into the space around you. Expand and feel all the space at once. Balance and hold your attention in expanded awareness of the space around you.

Imagine that you live in a universe of Radiant Light. Imagine this Light. Imagine the space around you filled with this Radiant Light.

Imagine your attention focused on and receiving this Radiant Light, imagine being filled with Radiance.

Feel yourself bathed, refreshed, and balanced in this Light

Sit with this peace for as long as you like. Tell yourself that you are refreshed and balanced and ready for your next activity in the day—or if it is bedtime, tell yourself that you are ready to have a restful, healing sleep.

Open your eyes and stretch. It is important to stretch after you have done any attention focusing practice meditation. Stretching allows tension and toxins to release.

Practice focusing your attention by noticing what is around you without passing judgment or commentary. Practice noticing what part of you is making the judgment. What part of you is reacting to the environment? Your mind? Your muscles? Your gut? Notice without commentary. Don't look for meaning. Don't interpret or evaluate. Don't analyze. Simply look without talking to yourself about looking. If you must interpret, analyze, evaluate, or comment do it without making a judgment. Practice not taking your environment personally.

Practice thinking in a new way. Practice noticing things in a new way. Stay alert to this.

RELAXATION: Do this each morning and each night before bed. Do it any time you feel stressed or tired. Be still, ask for silence and stillness, and breathe some deep (filling up the balloon) breaths, and as you quietly breathe, focus your attention on your hands and imagine Radiant Light pouring into your hands and filling your hands with Radiance. As your hands fill with light, practice radiant self-healing—brush your hands over your head, eyes, cheeks, throat (brush upward at your throat) and shoulders (brush across and down). If you like brush your arms, lower back, legs and feet, all the while asking for Radiant Light to assist you to relax and heal. Take as long as you like, finish and say "thank you."

WORD OF POWER PRACTICE: Each night before bed and each morning when you awaken repeat your "first waking thought" mantra.

Each morning, receive a Word of Power for that day and carry that Word with you.

POLARITY: When a challenge or problem comes up remember you are practicing a new approach to challenges and remember the Hermetic principle of polarity. Polarizing the problem helps you connect with and stay in touch with your real intentions. A polarity map on paper will be a constant reminder of where you want to focus your attention.

POWER POINTS: Utilize the Law of Reversal—practice power points. Remember—each moment is a vital moment. Practice utilizing the tremendous energy that is available to you in each moment of your life. Use power points to break the ego loop. Everytime you find yourself feeling vulnerable or victimized by lack, or making biased judgments, or feeling self-righteously angry and looking for who to blame, make it a power point and reverse it. Use your Words of Power to shift energy. Don't focus on the process in the moment, don't focus on *How*, focus on *What*. What is your true intention in this moment? Call it to you. Master the moment.

PERSONAL ACCOUNTABILITY: Pick a quality each day and repeat it during the day as a mantra. Keep a list of qualities and when you find yourself in an obsessive mind, reverse and recite your list of qualities, telling yourself that this quality is the truth about the existence you want. Keep a list of qualities on your altar. Suggested qualities:

Peace	Strength	Wisdom	Radiance
Patience	Flexibility	Balance	Freedom
Simplicity	Serenity	Discernment	Beauty
Spontaneity	Tolerance	Trust	Intelligence
Clarity	Courage	Humor	Surrender
Joy	Integrity	Grace	Passion
Compassion	Enthusiasm	Honor	Blessing
Acceptance	Gratitude	Make up your own	

ALTAR WORK: Creating an altar is a message to yourself that you mean it, that you are committed to your true existence, that you want it no matter what. There are no rules to follow when you set up an altar. It should represent the beauty of the qualities you would most like to embody, the kind of life you want to live and the kind of person you would most like to be, what is most true and beautiful to you. An altar can be a flower and a photo, a candle and a silk flower, a favorite picture and seashell that you carry around in a box. We carry altars in our hearts unconsciously in our memories of goodness and happiness. Create your altar in that same spirit. An altar creates a sacred space. It creates a framework of beauty for honoring your truth, your teachers, masters, or deities. It helps you set aside time to do a formal, devotional practice every day. A daily devotional practice creates a tremendous vortex of creative energy.

Within your sacred space you can create ceremonies for energizing and honoring your mantras—a Blessing Pot or some similar focused activity. You can sit at your altar, light a candle and write down your mantras and/or recite them. You can create or find a bead necklace and say your beads by reciting your mantras in the same way a Catholic recites a rosary. Write your mantras attentively. Speak your mantras attentively, with enthusiasm, passion and devotion. As if it matters—as if *you* matter. Keep all devotional work simple and light and imaginative. God is not ponderous. God is light, beautiful and harmonious. Do it lightly and say thank you.

FREEDOM: Notice belief. Belief is an idea or experience that you have incorporated into yourself as a deep emotional certainty. These certainties about life come from true experience (such as, "fire is hot and will burn; avoid fire . . . love hurt me, love is about pain, avoid love.") A certainty can be acquired by listening to others who have a strong impact on you, parents, peers, teachers. These deep certainties about life create your identity. A certain quality and similarity of beliefs create a belief system. A belief system creates many conditions. If you carry conditions you are not free. Once you've incorporated a condition it must be met if the system is to remain protected and intact. This means your belief system must be kept intact or your identity will not be safe. These conditions create many expectations that you constantly seek to fulfill. These expectations can become fixations. Fixation means an obsession with a fixed outcome and that only the outcome you are fixed on will satisfy your conditions and make you, safe, true, happy, and above all, *right.* This leads to an obsession with controlling your environment. A belief-oriented human being is an addictive, fear-driven, ego-centered human being. Choose to be truth oriented. Choose to be a peace-centered, love-centered, truth-centered, wisdom-centered, Creation-centered human being. This is Freedom.

Mantra for the rest of your life: "I Am Willing To Receive Blessing." Remember *you* are the polarity that is being transformed. You might experience an inner polarization of peace *and* anxiety simultaneously—waves of peace and waves of anxiety running through you at the same moment. Be patient. Don't condemn the anxiety—no self-condemnation—and don't forget to thank the peace.

Practice giving yourself the freedom to be wrong.
When in conflict choose to let go of conflict and ask Wisdom (Sophia) to come to you.
Notice Everything. Believe Nothing.
Plant a Patience Plant and do *not* watch it grow. Practice Radical Trust
Emulate your Soul. Plant a Spirit Rose.
Play a lot. Pray a lot. Love a lot. Say "thank you" a lot. Say "I love you".
Thank you, I love you, Walk in Beauty.

* * *

REVIEW: REPETITION—MAKING MAGIC

How do you make magic? You use the power of your attention at Point A in a mantra that declares your willingness to let go. You use the power of your attention at Point B in a Word of Power mantra that declares your new intention. The energy you create by utilizing the power of your attention and the power of intention sets up the conditions that allow change to happen.

If it is that easy, why is it so hard? Why doesn't it just happen? It actually is that simple but—your powerful attention is already focused. Your attention is fixed in old intentions, old programs of belief, fear, and instructions to yourself about what you can't have, mustn't do, have to do, have to be, have to have, etc. When you begin repeating a new and conscious intention your ego is energized *to resist the new intention.* This will make itself felt within you as accelerated fear or anger, even grief. You might feel frightened or very uncomfortable and you will have a strong desire to react, to fix it, to dominate your environment and bring your world back into safe focus. You might create a melodrama that keeps you processing some old hope or fear, something that worked in the past. What do you do then?

Practice radical trust. Keep in mind that you are re-structuring your self and this requires repeated practice. Keep in mind that your primal ego is the part of you that guards and guides your identity and it will not recognize a new intention as part of your identity. It resists. Your ego is a powerful part of your consciousness and one of its jobs is to resist change. So don't worry about resistance. Choose to proceed with your spiritual practices.

In undertaking this magical work of re-creating yourself you are profoundly altering your being. Your mind, your emotions, your very existence on earth is in the process of change. This is a spiritual process, a creative process that is very different than your old, linear, mental—*control* process. It will not feel familiar and safe. You must trust that your Spirit is in charge and your Spirit will take care of you. Your job now is the constant willingness to let go of fear, to let go of expectations, to let go of attachment to outcomes. Let go of trying to fulfill your ego's old blueprint for perfection and allow yourself to receive a new template for fulfillment.

Therefore, it is very important that you not try to judge your process or your progress. Let go of self-judgment and self-condemnation. Let go of processing your old stories about yourself as victim. Choose to replace your old stories with new stories that give you faith in the power of your Soul. Choose to direct the power of your attention to a mantra that defines everything you truly want. That mantra is "I Choose To Be True To Myself." Let go of trying to think your way to truth, let go of the how, of trying to control truth. Truth is always available and Truth cannot be rehearsed, it just shows up. Choose to be available to Truth and keep your door open. Then you will know what happiness is. Then you will sing Truth for the rest of your life. You will be a force for sanity and peace, for love and freedom, in the world. You will *be* God's dream come true. You will *be* true destiny, true intention. Then you will be The Great Work, the Holy Grail, the Philosophers' Stone. Then you will be your true, Essential Self.

CHAPTER 10

MASTERY: THE POWER OF DISCERNMENT

I AM OFTEN asked what results people can expect from taking the Course or from practicing any transformative path. I am also asked why, since the work is so hard and it is so easy to lose track of one's vision through so many changes, why even start, why bother to learn all this, why do it? I can't answer this for you. I don't know. For me there was no question; I simply did not want anything else. But often a person on a spiritual quest discovers halfway along the path that the search is hard, and they feel they want to quit, to get back to a place that in nostalgia, seems safe, and there comes a moment of crisis, a dark night of the Soul—like being halfway across the river and unable to see either bank. You might feel lost to one place and the other place seems a pipe-dream. And there is no safe place. Why begin it in the first place?

The search is hard because of our expectations. A spiritual search is not really a search because nothing is hidden, the path, in reality, consists of letting go of all of one's expectations about concepts like spiritual and search. Human beings are outcome oriented. Our primary life questions come from deep programming and are always in some form of "what's in it for me?" That is not a bad thing. You know what is in it for you or at least you know there is something in it that you want or you would not be questing. But spiritual longing is so intangible that the first thing you do on a spiritual path is look for some kind of certainty. And this is normal and all right. Your spiritual search begins with you wanting something visible and tangible, a feel good, a miracle, a specialness.

You begin with what is real to you at the moment you begin your search. People often begin their search with their attention focused on some unconscious beliefs about altruism, or on religious ideas about the ways in which manifesting and spirituality should look and should be expressed. This is energy that you eventually let go of. This is the energy of your expectations. This is the energy of judgment. Expect to experience discernment rather than judgment.

Real life change begins with where you are really at. You feel a lack. You want something. So you begin your trek. And you ask what can you expect to find. This is one of the unanswerable questions. You don't know until you're there and you learn when you are there that there is no "there." You begin with a willingness to let go, not knowing what you will be asked to let go of. You can expect to find your Essential Self. Whatever that means. You can expect to find expansion, delight, awe, and a new sense of who you are, why you are, and what you are.

It is just not possible to generalize about transformation, about a path of Light, about the *Great Work* because each individual has their own creative process. After years of teaching, I would say that what develops within each person is a greater ability to discern truth in the sense of knowing what is true for you *in each moment.* What develops is a taste for truth, a self-awareness that has more to do with *being* than with thinking. Awareness and discernment don't mean that you learn to *think* in a new way—you learn to *be* in a new way. Don't expect to replace one belief system with a newer up-to-date one. Expect to become less dependent on belief and more a person of faith. Expect to learn to trust in yourself.

What comes into being as you master these esoteric practices is self-knowledge and trust. A knowing that in each moment of your existence you can trust yourself because you are not trying to prove anything and no one has to prove anything to you. No one has to *get it.* Nothing has to happen, no conditions or expectations have to be fulfilled. Your integrity does not depend on the outside world. You don't need to depend on other people to prove who you are or validate who you are. True to yourself is who you are and you trust that.

This does not mean that you no longer make choices or hope for special outcomes. Hope can be inspiring. Hope can give your heart wings. But hope does not mean *attached to.* The secret of hope is to not be attached to an outcome.

Hope, without attachment to an *outcome,* means that you can allow yourself to feel inspired and hopeful of receiving what you are asking for but if you don't get it, if you don't get the response or the outcome from the world you'd hoped to get, it doesn't *faze* you because you are not attached to a particular thing having to happen in a particular way. You move on into each moment and each life experience with your creative trust unattached and unattacked.

You do not feel attacked because you do not take people or situations personally. You do not take conflict with people or situations with you into your future because you are not trying to prove that the person or situation is wrong and you are right. You do not have to defend your safety because you no longer feel unsafe. You easily receive because you are not attached to the receiving. You do not feel threatened by the future because you are capable of discerning truth in the moment. You have a love for truth and a new understanding of truth, an understanding that serves your higher purpose because it has no ulterior motive.

You have learned that truth cannot be rehearsed, truth is not something you can debate or prepare for, truth just appears. Truth is always available. You have chosen to be true to yourself, which means you have chosen to be *available* to truth and this has transformed any fear of truth within you. Truth always shows up when you need it because truth has always been present and truth will always be present.

What comes into being as you do your practices is a focused attention that is free of emotional attachment and emotional investment. You are free to discern truth and to respond creatively, fearlessly, spontaneously, and *appropriately* in each moment, no matter what challenges you are faced with. You are free because you are not personally attached to anything in that moment. You can move in any direction as you follow the movement of your Soul.

You can trust yourself to make truth available in the world. You can trust yourself to act with appropriate decision. You can trust that you see with the eyes of discernment. You can trust that you are a wisdom keeper, that a deep level of being true to yourself has manifested within you. You are at ease with who you are. You are free to be yourself. This kind of trust in yourself is mastery. This level of discernment, this depth of trust, creates a wisdom that does not come and go and that does not fail you when you need it. Discernment, wisdom, a knowing that stays constant is *mastery.*

Mastery is what you can expect from choosing to be true to your own wise, intelligent, true and loving humanity. Mastery is what you can expect from allowing your deliberate choices to create a path for you right into the heart of Consciousness itself. Mastering the moment is what you can expect. You no longer carry on a search for being "in the moment." You exist in what is. Each moment is free and true and you don't have to notice that you are living in the moment because you are so truly *being* in the moment.

Is this something you want? Does the longing for this kind of freedom keep resonating deep in your heart? Do you constantly feel that you lack something important, that if only you could find what it is you yearn for, life would be all wonderful? Do you want serenity? Would you like to let go of obstacles and encumbrance? What can you expect from practicing these spiritual practices? Why learn all this stuff? Why do it?

Do it for the miracle. Do it for the love. Do it for the Mystery.

Your freedom doesn't depend on having the right descriptions or definitions, or on understanding the right concepts. Your real life depends on having no concepts, no definitions, no descriptions, no attachments, no baggage. *Then* you are embraced by the Intelligence of God. Then the Beauty of God unfolds. The Mystery of God unfolds and you Walk in Gratitude and Beauty, true and effective in your world. Then you are the Holy Grail. Then you are God's lamp.

CHAPTER 11

EDITORIAL:

A VISION OF THE GREAT POLARITY

IMAGINE THAT EVERY human being who incarnates comes to this planet carrying a choice to be true to Creation. Imagine bringing to the world a consciousness that is free of conditions, free to act and move in joy and the wisdom of an understanding and loving human heart. Imagine bringing a wisdom that knows there is no wound so great it cannot be healed. A wisdom that understands that the human ego is not a terminally bad part of consciousness; it is a part of human consciousness that has been *wounded.*

I first heard the word "wound" in reference to the ego in the writings of Krishnamurti. My own revelations about w*ound* came from my desire to understand ego, what it is and why we have it. The ego is energy, a dimension of human *consciousness* that has awareness and purpose but which functions subtly, *energetically* and unconsciously rather than physically or consciously. It functions like an underground river, running beneath and influencing our seemingly reasonable judgments, motives, and actions. The egoic aspect of human consciousness runs through us and expresses in self-destructive or nihilistic ways only because it is *wounded.* And that wounded ego has come into being after countless human lifetimes of un-nurtured and mis-nurtured human beings. There is one wound—the belief that we are unloved. There is one word that will heal that wound. Love. To know how loved we are. Here is the great polarity—wounded love and unconditional love.

Unconscious and conscious. We are here to undertake the Great Work; to take what is unconscious and make it conscious, to take what is unloved and make it loved.

Imagine this. To transform wound into love is why each of us is here and why we keep coming back. We come here to take our own piece of un-consciousness and turn it into conscious awareness—to take our trash and turn it into treasure. *This is the alchemy of the heart.* The alchemy of the Soul. We come, incarnation after incarnation, carrying beliefs that have been forged for countless lifetimes. We come believing we are ego, believing that suffering is the truth about human life, believing that wounded love is real love.

Many of us are steeped in beliefs that evolved from reactions against the wound; religious beliefs proclaiming that existence is suffering, that suffering is inevitable, suffering is a judgment for original sin, suffering is a punishment, or suffering is redeeming and holy. We are taught that the wound is nasty, bad, and ugly, a punishment for our sins. We are taught that wounded or disfigured "others" are nasty and bad. We are taught to avoid the wound, condemn the wound, blame the wound, deny the wound, and above all, *fear* the wound. This keeps the wound moving in a continuous loop and the wounded ego continues to incarnate and suffer.

In writing the following story, I am sharing a vision that came to me in a meditation and illumined for me the difference between polarized consciousness and unpolarized consciousness—between wounded love and unconditional love. This vision reinforced my understanding of the Hermetic principles and my understanding of why it is important for me to teach. The vision begins with a view of polarized consciousness.

Imagine that the world is laid out as a great table and all the people who incarnate bring a gift to the table. Imagine that the gift that each person brings is the human potential for conscious awareness and the human ability to transmute energy. As incarnating humans come to the table of the world, they are, for the most part, bringing the eyes of their beliefs. They see with the eyes of their wound, and they bring to the table the shape of their beliefs, the shape of their past, the shape of their fear-derived, house-that-fear-built, ego.

Imagine that as each person comes to the table they learn to see it as contaminated in some way, each according to their belief system. They learn contamination. They learn to see contamination. Seeing contamination, they focus their attention on anti-contamination. These belief systems are founded on reactions against the wound.

A Christian looks with the eyes of belief . . . "the table is contaminated by sinners, heretics, and heathens."

A Jew looks . . . "the table has been contaminated by Gentiles."

A Muslim looks . . . "the table has been contaminated by infidels."

A Hindu looks . . . "the table has been contaminated by untouchables."

A Buddhist looks . . . "the table has been contaminated by suffering."

In essence, they focus on the same thing, on methods and strategies that will keep them separate from contamination, and that will transcend or destroy contamination, that will cleanse the table of the world. They are in an anti-contamination consciousness. They look at each other with judgment and blame rather than looking at the wound and seeing what is—seeing that the world is wounded and also beautiful. And that they are wounded and also beautiful. They don't look at each other and say "The table of the world is suffering from wounded love—what can we create that will heal wounded love?"

* * *

Every religion has an essential truth and beauty. Each one emphasizes good works according to religious law. And each came into being from prophets, avatars, and teachers, channeling God's Word in interpretations that were meant to speak to each particular culture. *Different lamps carrying the same essential Light.* So there are as many diverse religions as there are diverse and widely separated cultures. Each religion contains an anti-something. By "anti," I mean a reaction *against.* And that "anti" is focused on fixing and controlling the world rather than transforming and creating a brave new world.

Each religion came into being as a reaction against human suffering. Each religion contains beliefs that arose from a desire to control the state of the world, and each one is focused on a belief that the ego is the *satan*, i.e., the source of ignorance and suffering, and that the ego is dirty or bad, that suffering is an *inevitable* part of human existence, and that only belief in the particular religion one has given one's self to can save humanity from suffering and evil. Religion itself is based on a concept of original sin—of humankind as sinful *in its origins and original nature.*

The reality is that humans are *not* inherently sinful. Evil was created by the frightened and wounded human ego, terrified of lack and greedy in its obsession with *safety.* One of the most radical and welcome departures in religion today is Matthew Fox's book *Original Blessing* and the concept of Creation Spirituality.

Religious beliefs in outside, cosmic, dark forces, beliefs in the satan as responsible for human atrocity and madness, and beliefs in possession by evil others, have led to the belief that human beings must protect themselves from evil by *feeding* their various gods. This is the basis for sacrificial ceremonies. This belief has led to religious fatalism, a belief that evil is *cosmic*, so powerful that only the gods can fight evil. The belief that human beings are the *victims of* rather than the *creators of* evil has led to the practice of *scapegoating*—demonizing dangerous others and blaming them for the evils of the world.

Hitler is a dramatic twentieth-century example of scapegoating or demonizing. He demonized Jews and made them scapegoats for all the social evils in Germany at the time. Now, the Israeli Jews are scapegoating Palestinian Arabs. Scapegoating is *insatiable.* Slavery in America, which led to the demonizing of the African peoples, is another example. Scapegoating has become a *habitual* human reaction to pain—the demonizing of significant dark and dangerous others as the cause of suffering and evil.

The organized religions, Christianity and Buddhism, began as radical departures from the prevailing religious cultures. Jesus and Buddha, a carpenter and a prince, from separate and diverse cultures, called into action by God and reacting against the excesses of a previous orthodoxy, each within his own culture inspired a new spiritual path. Jesus and Buddha each refused to participate in beliefs and practices that separated human beings from the Source of love and wisdom. Both men were inspired by new concepts of wholeness and *personal accountability*. Both stressed kindness, charity, the search for wisdom, and compassionate action.

This was *radical.* Previous religious practices had been based on religious *law* and religious duty as defined by caste or class. At that time personal accountability was a new and radical concept. Each of these "new" men refused to do their calling in a spiritually correct way. They wandered the land teaching *anyone who wanted to learn*! Radical! This went against all the laws of caste and religious hierarchy. These men created a great planetary transformation. We are now in the midst of the next step of this radical planetary transformation. What are we going to create?

* * *

One Light, many lamps. The vision continues. Imagine these polarized, belief-ridden human beings, incarnating, arriving at the table of the world attached to the belief that *before* they can be free or saved, the ugly, unclean, suffering, dangerous world must be cleansed of all heathens, infidels, untouchables, of all pain, suffering, and dangerous others. This projection of fear and *withholding of love* and the limitations created by this separation from Love feeds the energy of the wounded ego. The human tendency to focus attention on an *anti*, to react against fear rather than move toward fearless peace, feeds more energy into the anti and strengthens the source of the reaction—strengthens the fear. Separation from Truth and the fearful distrust of Love has led to a world where scapegoating is used as a reasonable excuse for holy war and ethnic cleansing has reached monstrous proportions. And the leaders who promote ethnic cleansing and holy war, who promote any kind of war, are still looked at as leaders and not as insane examples of wounded love. And both the entertainment industry and the news media thrive on the monstrous worldviews that have been created by this *polarization* of human consciousness.

Imagine a vision of polarized consciousness spread out on the table of the world.

Now imagine the other side of the polarity. Imagine an unpolarized *consciousness that sees the wounded ego and its hallucinations through the eyes of Love.*

Jesus comes to the table of the world and looks at the wounded ego with the eyes of Love. Buddha comes to the table and looks with the eyes of Love.

Mohammed comes to the table and looks with the eyes of Love.

Sophia comes to the table and looks with the eyes of Love.

Kuan Yin comes to the table and looks at the wounded ego with the eyes of Love.

Isis comes to the table and looks with the eyes of Love.

Tara comes to the table and looks with the eyes of Love

Shakti comes to the table and looks with the eyes of Love.

Shiva comes to the table and looks with the eyes of Love.

Krishna comes to the table and looks with the eyes of Love.

On and on they appear and as they appear they blend into One Great Light.

All of them—the Light Beings, the Great Ones, the gods and goddesses, avatars, angels, devas, saints, crazy wisdom beings, all the free and true beings who have appeared as teachers in every culture on earth since the beginning of human time, come to the table. They bring the eyes of Love. They look at the human wound. They look at the wounded ego with compassion and wisdom.

They do not look at each other. They do not need to look at each other. They do not need to compete or compare. They do not need to dominate or submit. They do not need to find meaning. They do not need to conform or resist. They do not need to cooperate. They do not need to debate. They do not need to arrive at a consensus. They have no contradictions. They are unpolarized.

They have no quarrel with each other. Quarrel only exists in the wounded human ego. They have awareness. They see with One eye.

They drink from One Well of Love. They draw nourishment from One Radiant, Intelligent Light. They are Free.

They come to the table. Their vibrations merge into one great beam of Radiant Awareness. Their eyes of Love merge in a smile, a laugh, a song, a dance, a rejoicing. Their rejoicing resounds, calling the wounded ego into the dance of life. Their rejoicing resounds—re-sounds the Word throughout all Creation. And the Word transforms the wounded human ego and heals the wounded human heart.

Different lamps but the Light is the same. For centuries they have been coming. Spiritual genius. Teachers. Beings of Grace and Light. Hearer of Cries. Healing in Their Wings. Elegant and Eloquent they come. Diverse. Different lamps. One Light. Gratitude. Gratitude and Grace. Thank you, God.

* * *

Where are you in this polarity? Do you serve wound or Love? Where is your attention? The most crucial question in the universe is "what do you want?" Self-pity or self-realization? Melodrama or drama? Delusion or reality? Hallucination or vision? Quarrel or peace? Self-indulgence or strength? Dis-ease or health? Ignorance or intelligence? Victim or celebrant? Which Word is your master? Soul or ego? Grace or fear? Love? What are you willing to receive from Love? What are you willing to believe? You can believe anything you want. What do you want to receive? You receive what you have agreed to have. Are you agreeing to be wounded—to be a victim? Are you withholding Love? Do your choices come from reactions against the wound? Would you like to be true to yourself and create peace, strength, and wisdom in yourself and in the world?

Utilizing spiritual practices allows you to create immense amounts of energy, and *maintain* the movement of that energy toward truth. It takes immense amounts of energy to transmute the wounded ego. What are you *actually* doing when you transmute your old, wounded thoughts? You are transmuting the energy of wound that permeates and haunts the planet.

We, as we individually transform our own past, are literally transforming the planet. Believe it.

We transform the wounded planet by transforming our relationship with Love. How many times have you put out a begging bowl and expected Love to appear in it? How many one-way bargains have you tried, how many conditions have you demanded, as you stood before Creation with your begging bowl in your hand? *Don't put out a begging bowl and call it love.* Create Love by choosing to be true to yourself. Don't be a beggar for love. Don't beg. Don't be a victim. *Wisdom never begs.* If you keep begging, if you keep believing you need acceptance and validation according to the world's ego-centered criteria, *you will never feel real.* You will feel like a fraud. If you follow the path of being true to yourself, there will be Reality—authenticity, in whatever you accomplish for every part of your existence will be centered in truth.

We are inventing a world. *Consciously maintaining energy that moves toward truth is spiritual revolution.* This is not created through politics. It is created by individuals following the path of being true to their own highest desire for peace, their longing for freedom for all beings, their desire to create. *No matter what.* This is where the immense energy comes from and it is maintained in the human heart and moves and grows silently from heart to heart, person to person, until it becomes one Vast, Illumined Heart. One Light. One Dream. One Light—many lamps. Thank you.

BIBLIOGRAPHY FOR FURTHER STUDY

There are no books that I particularly recommend as reference books in the Course. Some of the books on this list are old favorites that I remember reading long ago, and some I include because they illustrate the diversity of the Western Esoteric genre. Some are out of print. Most of these books have bibliographies that will direct you to further studies. There are many fine recent books that I am not familiar with and there are books that I look at as old friends that I have not included. Since the path of alchemy is often a solitary path and there are many different beliefs and misconceptions within the esoteric world, the quality of information in that world ranges all the way from "Twilight Zone" to Superconscious Radiance. Be selective.

I am dividing this into four sections, Alchemy, Kabbalah, general books on Western Traditions, and Science.

ALCHEMY

Aromatico, Andrea. *Alchemy; The Great Secret. Harry N. Abrams Inc., 2000.*

Atwood, Mary Anne. *Hermetic Philosophy and Alchemy; A Suggestive Inquiry.* New York, Julian Press 1960. Reprint of an 1850 publication

Case, Paul Foster. *The True and Invisible Rosicrucian Order.* York Beach Samuel Weiser, 1985

Freke, Timothy and Peter Gandy. *The Hermetica; the Lost Wisdom of the Pharaohs.* Jeremy P. Tarcher/Putman, 1999.

Goddard, David. *The Tower of Alchemy; An Advanced Guide to the Great Work.* Weiser, 1999.

D'Avidla, Count Gablet. *The Mysteries of Eleusis* UK: Aquarian Press 1981. Reprint of an 1894 Edition.

Grossinger, Richard. *Alchemy: Pre-Egyptian Legacy, Millenial Promise.* Richmond, CA: North Atlantic Books 1979.

Hall, Manly P. Preface. *The Isiac Tablet, or, The Bembine Tablet of Isis.* By W. Wynn Westcott. Philosophical Research Society reprint of 1887 edition.

———. *Orders of the Great Work—Alchemy.* Philosophical Research Society

———. Introduction and commentary. *The Most Holy Trino Sophia of Comte De St.Germain.* The Philosophical Research Society Inc., 1983

———. *The Riddle of the Rosicrucians.* Philosophical Research Society pamphlet.

Lamy, Lucy. *The Mysteries of Ancient Egypt.* London, Thames and Hudson, 1981

Mead, G.R.S, Thrice-*Great Hermes, Three Volumes.* London, John R.Walkins, 1964. (1906)

Ramsay, Jay. *Alchemy: The Art of Transformation.* London, Harper Collins 1997

Shah, Indries Sayed. *Secret Lore of Alchemy; Oriental Magic.* London: Rider and Co., 1956

Three Initiates. *The Kybalion: Hermetic Philosophy of Ancient Egypt and Greece.* Chicago: Yoga Publication Society, 1936

Yates, Frances. *The Rosicrucian Enlightenment.* Shambhala Publications, 1978.

———. *Giordano Bruno and the Hermetic Tradition.* University of Chicago Press 1964.

KABBALAH

Cooper, David A. *God is a Verb: Kabbalah and the Practice of Mystical Judaism.* Riverhead Books, 1997.

Epstein, Perle *Kabbalah: The Way of the Jewish Mystic.* Garden City, NY: Doubleday 1978.

Fortune, Dion. *The Mystical Quabala.* Published by Ernst Benn Ltd., 1970

Hoffman, Edward. *The Kabbalah Deck; Pathway to the Soul.* Chronicle Books. 2000

Knight, Gareth. *Practical Guide to Quabalistic Symbolism—2 vol.* Samuel Weiser, 1978.

Leet, Leonora. *The Secret Doctrine of the Kabbalah: Recovering the Key to Hebraic Sacred Science.* Inner Traditions, 1999.

Mathers S.L. McGregor *The Kabbalah Unveiled* 1887 reprint NY: Weiser, 1974.

Regardie, Israel *The Tree of Life: A Study in Magic.* NY Samuel Weiser, 1969.

Williams-Heller, Ann. *Kabbalah, Your Path to Inner Freedom.* Quest Books/Theosophical Publishing Co. 1990.

WESTERN SPIRITUAL TRADITIONS—GENERAL

Ashcroft-Nowicki, Dolores. *The Initiate's Book of Pathworkings.* Aquarian Press 1985.

Bailey, Alice. *The Consciousness of the Atom* New York, Lucien Trust 1924—*any of hers*

Bessant, Annie. *Thought Power* London: Theosophical Publishing House, 1922.—*same*

Bessant, Annie and C.W. Leadbeater. *Thought Forms.* Adyar, India, Theosophical 1925.—*any of their Theosophical Books are interesting.*

Blavatsky, H.P. *The Secret Doctrine; Centennial Edition.* Two Volumes. London: Theosophical Publishing House. 1988 reprint of the original 1888 edition.

______. *Isis Unveiled.* Two Volumes. Theosophical Publishing House *Madame Blavatsky is the mother of the Western Esoteric Tradition. Her books have many reprints*

Bonewits Isaac. *Real Magic* York Beach, ME, Samuel Weiser, 1989.

Butler, W.E. *Lords of Light: The Path of Initiation in the Western Mysteries,* Rochester, VT Destiny Books 1990

______. *The Magician: His Training and Work.* London: Aquarian Press.

Case, Paul Foster. *The Tarot; A Key to the Wisdom of the Ages.* NY: Macoy Publishing, 1947 Los Angeles: Builders of the Adytum, 1990

Corbin, H. *Creative Imagination in the Sufism of Ibn Aragbi;* trans. Mannheim, R. Princton U Press 1969, Princeton, NJ

Dzielska, Maria. Translated by F. Lyra. *Hypatia of Alexandria.* Harvard U. Press, 1995

Fortune, Dion. *Applied Magic.* Aquarian Press, 1979.

———. *Aspects of Occultism.* London: Society of the Inner Light, 1962.

———. *The Circuit of Force.* Thoth, 1983.

———. *The Cosmic Doctrine.* Aquarian Press, 1976

———. *Esoteric Orders and Their Work.* Llewellyn Press, 1978

———. *The Training and Work of an Initiate.* London: Society of the Inner Light, 1967.

Fox, Matthew. *Original Blessing, A Primer in Creation Spirituality.* Bear & Co. NM, 1983

Fritz, Robert. *The Path of Least Resistance.* Stillpoint Publishing, 1984.

Giles, Cynthia. *The Tarot; History, Mystery, and Lore.* Fireside, 1994

Godwin, J. *Mystery Religions and the Ancient World.* London, Thames & Hudson, 1981

Green, Marian. *The Path Through the Labyrinth.* Thoth Publications

Griscom, Chris. *Ecstasy Is A New Frequency; Teachings of the Light Institute.* Fireside Bks., Simon & Schuster 1987.

Hall, Manly P. *The Adepts in the Esoteric Classical Tradition: Part Two; Mystics and Mysteries of Alexandria.* The Philosophical Research Society, Inc., 1988.

———. *The Secret Teachings of All Ages, An Encyclopedic Outline of Masonic,Hermetic, Quabbalistic, and Rosicrucian Symbolic Philosophy.* The Philosophical Research Society 1969.

———. *The Wisdom of the Knowing Ones, Gnosticism: The Key to Esoteric Christianity.* The Philosophical Research Society.

Inayat Khan, Hazrat. *The Unity of Religious Ideals,* NY: Sufi Order Publications, 1978

King, Serge. *Kahuna Healing.* Wheaton, Ill. Theosophical Publishing Co 1983

Krishnamurti—I recommend anything of his.

Leadbeater, C.W. *The Masters and the Path* Adyr, India; Theosophical Pub House 1925.

Lethbridge, T.E. *Witches.* NY: The Citadel Press, 1968.

Leivgoed, B.C,J. *Mystery Streams in Europe and the New Mysteries,* Anthroposophic Press 1982

Levi, Eliaphas. *Transcendental Magic.* Trans. By Waite. London: Rider and Co., 1968.

______. *Key of the Mysteries.* Trans by Crowley. London: Rider and Co, 1969.

Lindholm, Lars B. *Pilgrims of the Night; Pathfinders of the Magical Way.* Llewellyn Publications.

Long, Max Freeman. *The Secret Science at Work.* De Vorss, 1953.

______. *The Secret Science Behind Miracles.* Los Angeles: Kosmon Press 1948.

Maeterlinck, Maurice. *The Great Secret.* New York. Citadel Press 1969

Matthews, Caitlin. *Sophia: Goddess of Wisdom; The Divine Feminine.* Harper Collins, 1991.

Mattews, Caitlin and John. *Mabon and the Mysteries of Britain.* Penguin/Arkana 1987.

______. *The Western Way, Vol.2: The Hermetic Tradition* Penguin/ Arkana 1985-1986.

Regardie, Israel. *Golden Dawn; History of a Secret Society.* Llewellyn

Satprem, The Mother at Aurobindo. *The Mind of the Cells; or Willed Mutation of the Species.* Translated from the French by Venet, Luc. Institute for Evolutionary Research. Mt.

Vernon, WA. 1972. Reprint of 1881 French edition.

Schaup, Susanne. *Sophia: Aspects of the Divine Feminine.* Samuel Weiser. 1997

Schipflinger, Thomas. *Sophia-Maria, A Holistic Vision of Creation.* York Beach, ME. Samuel Weiser 1998.

Schwaller De Lubicz, Isha. *The Opening of the Way: A Practical Guide to the Wisdom of Ancient Egypt.* Inner Traditions International, 1981.

Schwaller De Lubicz, R.A. *Sacred Science,* NY Inner Traditions Int. 1982

______. *Symbol and Symbolic: Egypt, Science, and the Evolution of Consciousness.* Autumn Press, 1978.

Smoley, Richard and Jay Kinney. *Hidden Wisdom; A Guide to the Western Inner Traditions.*Penguin/Arkana, 1999.

Spangler, David. *The Laws of Manifestation.* Findhorn Publications, 1981.

Sri Aurobindo, *The Essential Aurobindo.* Edited by McDermott, Robert. New York, Schocken Books, 1973.

Sri Aurobindo, *The Hidden Forces of Life.* Compiled by Dalal, A. S. Sri Aurobindo Ashram Press, by Sri Aurobindo Ashram Trust. Pondicherry, India 1990.

Steiner, Rudolph. *Evolution and Consciousness.* London, Rudolph Steiner Press, 1979

______. *Occult Science, An Outline.* London, Rudolph Steiner Press, 1979

______. *The Search for the New Isis; The Divine Sophia.* Spring Valley, NY, Mercury Pr. 1983.

Tuttle, Paul. Channeling "Raj", *You Are the Answer; A Journey of Awakening.* Kairos Inc. Seattle, WA. 1985

SCIENCE

Video: *Fractals: The Colors Of Infinity.* Films For The Humanities & Sciences. Princton, NJ.1994

Briggs, John. *Fractals; The Patterns of Chaos.* NY: Touchstone, 1992

Capra, Fritjof. *The Tao of Physics.* Boston: Shambhala, 1975.

______. *The Web of Life.* Anchor/Doubleday, 1996.

Gleick, James. *Chaos: Making a New Science.* NY: Viking, 1987.

61287954R00086

Made in the USA
San Bernardino, CA
14 December 2017